A Widow's Pilgrimage

A WIDOW'S PILGRIMAGE

by Jean Hersey

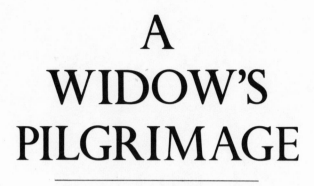

CONTINUUM
New York

Second Printing

1980
The Continuum Publishing Corporation
815 Second Avenue, New York, N.Y. 10017

Library of Congress Cataloging in Publication Data
Hersey, Jean, 1902–   A widow's pilgrimage.
1. Hersey, Jean, 1902–   2. Widows—United
States—Biography.   I. Title.
HQ1058.5.U5H47   301.42'86'0924   79-16776   ISBN 0-8264-0030-2

Gratefull acknowledgment is made to Elizabeth Gray Vining for permission to quote from
Quiet Pilgrimage.

For Bob
Remembering with deepening joy
our fifty happy years together

Foreword

When Jean Hersey's husband died I read whatever books I could lay my hands on that described the phases of recovery from grief in order to learn how I could help. As the weeks passed and Jean began her painful steps down a new lonely path, the dos and don'ts in these books emerged into reality. Here are some of them I found helpful: Behave in a matter-of-fact manner. Talk simply and frankly. Don't avoid discussing the person who has died; often that is what the griever most craves. Use common terms—"He died," not euphemisms such as "He passed on." Don't offer advice; and don't criticize. This is a time when the individual's self-confidence is at its nadir, and both advice and criticism can only harm. Don't set a time limit on the bereaved's recovery. Just be patient. Above all, listen—receptively.

One of the books I read offered this advice to the griever: try to find just one person in whom you can confide your innermost feelings and thoughts. Someone who will not sit in judgment; someone who will listen with understanding sympathy. This is the role I gradually came to play in Jean's life. It has been a growing experience for me, challenging and rewarding. I feel privileged to have been the person called on to respond to Jean in her hour of need.

Jane

The First Year

March 16

Our flowering crab beside the terrace is especially full of buds this year. This is one of Bob's particular favorites. It blooms for several weeks in the spring, and then in late summer swings charming little red crab apples over the branches. March is a lovely time in Tryon. The dogwood everywhere and the redbud are about to open, azaleas are showing color, daffodils are blooming all over the place, and the air is balmy with spring. Our little enclosed garden will be a paradise of bloom in another week or two.

In a few minutes we will drive to the airport. Meanwhile, we walk through the garden to see the fruits of Bob's labors of yesterday. He had made a small vegetable plot in a sunny spot at the far end of the garden. He leveled a slope, turned in several wheelbarrow loads of rich black compost. He next surrounded the space with chicken-wire fence to keep out neighboring dogs that, I have found, love to stretch out prone on tender young lettuce or else tunnel under the plants.

Now, before leaving, we wandered out to admire the newly completed area.

"I don't believe we ever had so many buds on the flowering crab," Bob said as we moved past it. It was really burgeoning. He reached out and touched fondly a cluster of pink buds, still tiny, but pink as could be—almost scarlet. Then we stood a few moments admiring the vegetable garden-to-be.

"We can have beans and lettuce," I said.

"And tomatoes," Bob added. "I'll cut some saplings in the woods for stakes when I get back."

As we turned out of our drive heading for the airport we checked over last-minute details.

"One thing I didn't do," Bob said. "Send a check to confirm our reservations for the cruise. Will you send it?"

"Yes, indeed, I will," I responded in a glow, merely to think of it. We were going on a Caribbean seminar cruise in April, and our check would confirm the reservations.

This present trip of Bob's was the first time he and I had been separated for a few years. I felt as if he were heading for the moon. It seemed a momentous departure.

What a beautiful drive to the airport. Everywhere fields were green—here and there men were plowing. The peach orchards on both sides of the road were in full flower—a gentle, delicate pink against the backdrop of the blue mountains. Hogback, Rocky Spur, Melrose, all our favorites lined up in a many-peaked silhouette against a very blue sky.

At the airport, as Bob lifted his suitcase out of the car, I marveled again at how lightly he always travels, one suitcase for his clothes and the grandchildren's presents. He was heading for California to visit our two sons, Bob and Tim, and their families, one in Sacramento and the other in San Francisco.

We had decided I wouldn't go with him. I had had the flu and, while now over it, mostly, it seemed best that I stay home and get completely well. He would have a lovely experience visiting the children and grandchildren, and come back filled with tales of good family times.

I would finish gathering energy. We would celebrate Easter at home together, and then there would be the cruise.

The airport was busy and bustling—the azaleas in the garden there were also budding, and the fountains playing. It was one of those days when the world sings, and something in you responds with a little inner tune. They announced the flight; we embraced warmly. I would miss my husband for these next ten days. I waved him off as he merged with a group of other passengers. Then I waited to see him climb the plane's steps before turning back toward the car.

I, too, had plans—ten days of them. I was going to give the house a good spring cleaning, turning out cupboards and closets. I would catch up at my desk and be all ready for a gala Easter when Bob returned.

One special plan I had. Bob's study was a little grimy and needed repainting. I had secretly arranged to have this done while he was away so it would be waiting as a surprise when he returned.

Already, driving away from the airport, I began to think of the joy of Bob's return.

Back home, the mail had come—nothing interesting—just a batch of those things I never understand that come in the mail and that I always put on Bob's desk. Insurance letters, communications from the income-tax man and the government and other mysterious places. Bob always tends to such matters in our life, and they are dark and unknown areas to me—not a part of my world.

I have merely a very simple household budget, but checkbooks and such Bob understands and resolves, and all business matters, as he has always done for the fifty years we have been married.

It will be fifty years this year, and we have been thinking about having a family celebration later on in the fall when our anniversary arrives. Wouldn't it be wonderful, we keep telling each other, if the children and grandchildren could all come and be with us? This is something we are beginning to envision. It will be next December.

The day passed in pleasant ruminations. As I sat down to one lonely lamb chop and as an evening of being by myself stretched before me I was already looking forward to Bob's return. What a pleasure that will be, I thought. I began dreaming of our Easter together, our cruise. We have a lot to look forward to—a great deal going for us in a general way. We love our new house and the new community we have moved to and lived in now for nearly seven years. We enjoy our new friends and neighbors. We have much ahead of us and a good life, I thought drowsily, as I drifted off to sleep.

March 28
March 28—that date is seared into my memory and will be, I believe, forever. Good Friday, with nature smiling and all the world preparing for a happy Easter.

It was sunny and warm, the garden path was bordered in primroses in all colors—the redbud and dogwood were almost full out on our place and all around Tryon, edging roads everywhere and through the woods. The mountains were covered in white drifts where the dogwood flowered. A blanket of wild iris folded up around our little garden pool, and three yellow tulips rose up beside an old stump there.

Even before I fully wakened I had that lovely feeling that something great was happening—that feeling of joy while you are still on the borders of sleep. As I opened my eyes I remembered. This was the day Bob was to come home. I would meet his plane this afternoon.

I was planning a gala roast-beef dinner for him, and I would arrange flowers everywhere, and some of the purple clematis from the fence for the dining-table centerpiece. I must be up and stirring. And so the day began. I drifted in a haze of happiness through Cowan's Supermarket, buying this and that and, with a two-rib roast, settled in the car and headed for home.

Why was I so terribly excited? Bob had been away for ten days or so before many times. I had had several phone conversations with him since he left, and again one last night. He had told me what he was doing, and I had caught him up on my activities. Most of them. I hadn't told him about my encounter with the fire hydrant. Since we moved to Tryon we reduced our car number from two to one. No need here for two cars. Whenever we went anywhere Bob always drove. I drove very little, and these years in the south I had become rather out of practice. The day after Bob left I went shopping in the pouring rain and did a multitude of errands. As I drove home I was congratulating myself on getting in and out of a number of parking places with no problem. Turning in our drive with a sigh of relief I encountered the hydrant with a wham, scraping the side of the car by the door and leaving a great indentation and ugly gash the full length of the car. I was ashamed. How could I be so stupid?

No use to worry Bob about this long-distance, so I hadn't mentioned it at all. The body shop would fix the car, but they couldn't take it for another couple of weeks. Bob would see it when he got home and good-naturedly tell me not to worry.

It was great talking with him on the phone. He sounded so warm and near. He has a wonderful voice anyway. Last night he called to say he was all packed up and ready to catch the ten o'clock plane in the morning, and this was the gala day. I had had a fine ten days getting Bob's room repainted, driving to Spartanburg to shop for a suit to wear on the cruise and some dresses, including one lovely, long, yellow chiffon for dinner on the ship.

I picked some of the first azaleas for the living room; some wild iris for the bathroom. The flowering crab was opening. I put some blossoms on Bob's dresser. The three tulips I would leave. They looked so sunny and gay. I floated three large, deep-purple clematis and a few leaves in a silver bowl on the dining table.

I sat down to a lunch of macaroni and cheese and salad. Halfway through the meal the doorbell rang. Through the window, to my amazement, I saw our minister. He never came in the middle of the day. I hoped everything was all right. His wife, a very dear friend of mine, had been quite sick. Was she all right, I wondered?

I opened the door.

"Well, hello," I said cheerily. "Do come in. I'm just eating lunch. Won't you have some macaroni and cheese with me?"

He didn't answer—how unlike him.

"Come into the living room and sit down, Jean," he said rather solemnly. "I need to talk to you." Where was his usual smile and twinkle?

Could it be something about his wife? She had been in and out of the hospital. Perhaps she was in again—oh dear. They had had such trouble, I thought, as I passed into the living room and sat down on the sofa. Our minister sat beside me. He took my hand.

"Jean, Bob died in his sleep last night," were the words he spoke. The next thing I knew I was weeping on his shoulder. "And," he continued, "Joan will be here at five o'clock this afternoon." Joan is our daughter.

Something died in me at that moment, something that was a part of the essence of me. I stopped weeping and heard my voice say, as from a great distance, "What happened?"

Our son, Bob, had gone to wake his father to take him to the airport, surprised that he wasn't already up, since he always woke early. He found him lying in bed peacefully as if asleep.

"But he couldn't have died. I just talked to him last night and he was perfectly well."

Through the haze I heard our minister say, "Bob was seventy-seven years old, Jean, and he died in the way that is the very best way for all of us to go when our time comes."

There seemed to be a screen between me and the man before me. He seemed to be talking from a long way off. He told me that our son, Bob, had telephoned Joan. Dear Joan, who didn't want me to hear the news on the phone.

So she had called our minister and asked him if he would tell me.

Actually, I later learned, Joan was on the way out the door, suitcase in hand, when her phone rang. She was going to catch the train to spend Easter with her son and daughter-in-law in New Hampshire. One minute later and she would have been gone, and no way to reach her until Monday.

I am so hazy about the rest of that day. I don't know how people knew so soon, but they began to come, close friends, and two couples we knew well. I greeted them, embraced them, cried a little, thanked them for coming. I must have said something, but I don't know what.

Some of the time I was sitting on the sofa in the living room. People were roaming in and out of the kitchen. The smell of coffee filled the air. People were standing around with cups and saucers in hand.

I don't remember people coming. They were just there, all around me, those I loved the most and knew the best since we had moved down here. At one point I remember lying down in the bedroom, and two or three friends came in, so I wasn't alone. I heard my voice at times, but I don't know what I said.

What would life be without dear friends? I remember sitting in bed eating the rest of my macaroni automatically. I couldn't taste it. I don't know why I felt I must eat it, but I did. One friend said, "I have a tray for eating in bed I'll bring to you if you like."

"But I won't be eating in bed," I replied. "In fact, I will get up now."

Someone arranged about meeting Joan. Homer and John, close friends and neighbors, went to the airport to meet her. The house was still full of people when she arrived. Through some vague sense of voices a few moments stand out. There was Joan coming in the front door into the living room. We were in each other's arms. Both of us were weeping, yet at the same time, strangely, strengthening each other. It was wonderful to have her.

"Bob and Tim will come tomorrow," Joan said. Someone must call my sister-in-law and her husband—Kay and Del. Joan did. They would also come tomorrow. Homer would give them his apartment to stay in while they were here.

All the while, the flowering crab stood outside, opening buds into the gentle spring air. The dogwood glowed in pink and white. The redbud swept its tones of dusty lavender through the woods. From time to time I glanced out the window at spring, the spring Bob would not see, or would he? I looked around at my friends; I couldn't seem to relate to them, yet I felt a great wave of support coming up through those who were there. I felt another wave of support drifting in the window from the beauty outside. Yet I didn't want to go on. I just wanted to sink down and go under.

Joan took over in the kitchen, and there was a meal—supper. A few people stayed. They were talking about everyday subjects. It was all too much for me. I excused myself and went into the bedroom. Joan followed me.

And then I began to cry. It was as if a dam broke. I could not stop. Joan put her arms around me. After a while I did stop. Nothing was any different from when I had started. I felt just as awful. The bottom had dropped out of my world—my life was over—and crying did no good. People said it did—I remember. If crying did no good there was no use in it. I had better carry on with what needed doing. Funny, my life is over, and yet I am still alive and here. How is that? I guess I am not making any sense. As from a great distance, I heard Joan speak.

She said, "To only very special people is it given to go on Good Friday, Mother. Father was a very special person."

I sat there a while, numb with pain that wasn't physical. Then I had my first coherent thought. I realized that Joan was suffering the loss of a beloved father whom she had always loved and been close to. How selfish I was being, not thinking of her loss, and this would be true of Bob and Tim, and Kay and Del when they arrived, too. I must try not to think of myself.

Meanwhile, Joan was sustaining me, and I must lend her strength. How could I lend anyone strength at this point, when I had so little myself?

I had another coherent thought. Why hadn't I gone with Bob on the trip west? I never should have let him go alone. How could I have let him go alone at his age? If I had gone with him, he might not have died. How terrible and how guilty I felt. I began telling all this to Joan. I lay down on the bed and began to cry again. Maybe crying got you nowhere, but it just welled up, and I let it come. I really wanted to give up, to give over, to have this terrible nightmare I was in go away. But no such thing happened. The nightmare is reality, is the way things are, and I am deep in it. No escaping the facts. Bob is gone, and I'll never see him again.

Mingled with the sense of tragedy and deadness that filled me, mingled with the feeling of guilt that I hadn't gone west, was the sense of love coming from Joan. I could feel it coming to me in waves. What do people do in crises who don't have children? You take care of them when they are little. They lean on you. When you get older the relationship changes; they take care of you, you depend on them.

"I am going to give you a nice back rub," Joan said. "First, you're going to take a warm bath."

After the bath I lay in bed, neither awake nor asleep, but in that same weird state of being emotionally dead but physically alive. Joan gave me a beautiful back rub. This is something we have always done for each other in times of stress.

Afterward, all was quiet. Joan turned out the light and left me, and as she closed the door the hall light shown in and, for an instant, caught in its beam the bouquet of flowering crabapple blossoms on Bob's dresser. Then all was dark.

How alone I felt.

March 29, 30, 31

These three days seem to merge into a long, endless stretch of time, a single day without end, a day of pain that never let up. The three days are a blur to me, a blue haze of people calling, the doorbell ringing, phone calls coming from all over, and people arriving to be helpful and impart love and warmth. Some I speak with, some I cannot.

Homer met Bob and Tim in the afternoon of Easter Saturday. It was a blessing to have the three children, now adult men and woman with their own partly grown families. Then Kay and Del arrived, bringing their special love and caring. There were meals to get and to eat. I moved, I did things, but I was numb. People began bringing food: casseroles, roasts, cake, custard. Mr. Cowan, at the supermarket, sent a roast ham, still hot. We ate it for dinner Saturday night. The refrigerator was full—how dear people can be, neighbors, friends. And now flowers began to come from family and friends in far places. The house was soon filled with them. Through a haze of faces, now and then one would stand out clearly, now another. Everything seemed taken out of my hands. Other people were answering the phone and the door. Letters of sympathy began to come. Joan, the boys, and I read them, appreciative of people's love, of their expressions of understanding.

We must plan the memorial service for Tuesday. Our minister came, and we quietly discussed these things.

Business matters must be tended to. Bob and Tim went through their father's clothes, sorting and taking some of the things they could wear. I was happy that they could use them. They went over business matters. How could I ever handle these things? They found me a lawyer to whom I could turn with the mail I didn't understand. They took me to the bank that Bob had dealt with, where I met and talked with the people with whom I shall do business. We talked about the things I will have to learn about. And all the time I felt I wasn't there. And there was a persistent hammering in my brain, beating out the words, "Bob is gone, you won't ever see him again. You are alone now."

Nights I lay alone imagining Bob in the bed alongside mine. Once, in the starlight coming through the window, I thought I saw him lying there. I had pushed the quilted bedspread back from my bed onto his, and it lay rumpled up, forming the shape of a person and reminding me of the many nights Bob and I had shared the two beds close together.

All night I was thinking I heard him turning over, imagining I heard him speak to me. Dreaming of him in the few snatches of sleep I got. If only I could die, too, die as he had—just not wake up tomorrow. I pray to die. My life is nothing without him. I cannot face going on. I don't want to go on. Why, dear God, must I?

How could I possibly learn to live alone after fifty years of being together? I had never made a decision without Bob. I was not even half a person without him. I couldn't even balance a checkbook and get it to come out right.

And all the while the fragrance of spring blew in the open windows—the dogwood unfolded, stretching its blossoms wide. Little steeples of ajuga marched along the terrace up to our small garden pool. The myrtle bloomed beside the pink candy-striped tulips. The whole world of nature sparkled, but I had no connection with any of this. My world was over. My life had ended on Good Friday morning.

April 1
There was the service itself. I sat with Bob on my right and Tim on my left. Joan played a solo on the recorder from up behind the choir stalls—the *William Tell* Overture, by Rossini. The clear tone of the recorder was perfectly beautiful as it echoed through the tall nave of the church. There were white snapdragons on the altar. Now they were playing "Greensleeves," one of the pieces of music we had chosen. The church was full. The Ro-

tary Club occupied a large section. Friends filled the rest. A friend read Bob's favorite poem, "The Birches," by Robert Frost, as part of the service. It was a lovely service. From a distance I watched myself move, get up and sit down, heard myself sing. But I really wasn't there at all.

I was walking in our garden with Bob just before he left. Now we are in the living room, and he has just lit a fire in the grate, using the wood he had cut and stacked this past winter. I am hooking my rug, and Bob is reading aloud to me. We are reading Delderfield's book, Give Us This Day. *It was on the table now in the living room, where Bob had closed it when he finished reading it that last night. I am serving dinner, and we are sitting by candlelight eating together, he and I. We are walking through the spring woodland together.*

When the service was over, we moved into the Common Room, stood in line, the four of us, Joan, Bob, Tim and I—receiving people as they came to express their sympathy. I greeted friends. I spoke to each one, but it was someone else speaking.

"Yes, we did have a wonderful life together—I do have countless good memories—you were so kind to come— yes, there was no problem, he just died—thank you for all you have done—the casserole was marvelous. I do appreciate your being here—indeed, it was thoughtful of you."

I was touched by the caring and concern of my friends. The memorial service was lovely, if anything could be said to be lovely that week. But I was somewhere else— climbing the Alps with Bob, swimming on the beach at Cape Cod.

Moments out of the past, peak moments kept crowding

in, each to be relived briefly and cherished, and then let go of so another could take its place.

People kept coming up to the four of us. "Thank you so much for the cake. We shall enjoy it—it was thoughtful of you to drive so far to come today—we all appreciate it."

And so we left the church and came home to a house filled with flowers that sent their fragrance through the rooms. A new pile of letters had come. Letters from far and near.

"Shall we light the fire?" our son, Bob, asked. Bob Senior had laid the fire for me to enjoy while he was away and I was alone. I hadn't burned it. Now we sat in the living room and watched the flames curl up over the logs Bob had first so carefully cut and stacked out at the end of the garden and then arranged in the grate.

Bob's last fire.

April 3
The children all left today, and I shall miss them. I just threw away the crab apple blossoms on Bob's dresser. They have been beautiful, but are dropping now. They were yesterday, and I must try to live in today and tomorrow. I put white azaleas there instead. I think I shall keep fresh flowers on Bob's dresser for a while at least. I like to come in the room and see them. They are like the sun trying to break through the black clouds of my days.

My life seems to have shattered into a thousand pieces. Now I must pick up the shards one by one and put them together into a totally new pattern. How will they fit? Can I fit them together? Can I possibly find the new shape, and how? I don't think I can. But I have to. It has been said that nothing comes to us but with it comes the strength to take it, weather it, stand up to it, and make something constructive out of it.

April 8

When crises and tragedy come you live for days at the core and center of life. Trivialities fall away. Truths stand naked and bare. The nitty-gritty facts of life are before you to cope with.

You surprise yourself when you see what your guts are made of, what comes from your depths to help you stand firm and steady and at your center. Other people's confidence and faith in you help you enormously, are some things that sustain you.

Trivialities are important, vital, too, and have their place, but often in ordinary living we spend more time than need be with them. Crises tell us, come and be more at your center in your thinking, feeling, and being. It needn't be always stark and awful happenings that draw you to your center, but peak experiences, too, and sometimes merely a quiet thoughtfulness.

An hour later I wonder where I got that strength, those guts, because I feel made of jelly and unable to face a single person at the door asking directions for the neighbor up the street. This is how it is for me. One hour I can stand firm, the next hour I cannot.

April 9

I am now alone—so very alone. I am sitting out on the terrace answering letters. Many come each day as more and more old friends hear the news about Bob and write me their sympathy.

"Thank you so much for your kindness and thoughts of me," I write. "Your letter was wonderful, and such a help." They all were helpful, all expressions of thoughtfulness on the part of friends were appreciated. It was difficult to keep my mind on what I was doing sitting there on the terrace. Now, in the distance I hear the lovely sound of Bob cutting wood. Perhaps he is sawing logs, or maybe chopping kindling at the old stump he keeps for the purpose. Now I see him laying and lighting a fire. Nobody builds a fire as easily and skillfully as Bob does. I loved to watch him.

All the while, spring is unfolding more each moment, the air warms, flowers burgeon; I look at them and find it hard to care. I walk in the garden alone. Flowers and all that grows have always been an elixir to me, a source of strength and refreshment, but not now. I am able to feel nothing. Someone said I was in a state of shock. Maybe. It was like nothing I had experienced before.

One day I walked out to see the little vegetable garden and plant some beans in it—a friend had given me special bean seeds. As I was planting I began wondering, did Bob overdo when he was digging and making this garden so recently? He has always dug, turned the earth, and planted. But perhaps I should have slowed him down on this, coaxed him to stop. Can this awful thing that has happened be my fault? What should I have done differently?

Something deep inside me tells me that when it is your time to go you go. I hear these words, and yet continue to feel guilty, and wonder what I should have done differently to change the circumstances.

You could not change the circumstances, the voice of

inner knowing tells me. You need to accept what is. It is useless to feel guilty. Maybe so, but I do all the same. I argue with my inner self.

It seems ages since the children left, yet it is only five days. I am alone, and feeling terribly bereft. I am asked to dinner here and there. I go, and am there in body, but not in spirit. I am thinking of Bob day after day, and worse, night after night, while I sleep very little.

I start to set the table one evening for my dinner alone, and automatically I set two places.

April 10

This morning I wakened quite disgusted with myself. Many people have lost husbands. It was not something to lay you out flat about. It was a challenge to meet. Even as I said this to myself I felt I couldn't meet it. I am older and so much less resilient now. I cannot seem to care to make the effort to meet this situation.

"Oh yes, you can," something in me said.

"But how?"

"You will know." But I don't know.

How lucky I had been to have had fifty years with Bob, and such a fifty years. We had had our peaks and our dips, as in all lives, but all told, we had been very lucky. I had my memories, I told myself sternly. But I am finding gratitude and memories aren't enough on which to build a new life.

It is a brand new and so different life I need to build. Joan, the day before she left, helped me with an outline of a day. These are some of the simple rules she and I puzzled out together.

Ingredients for Each New Day

1. Meditation and exercises every morning. (I do these anyway.)

2. Walk a mile. (Don't go in the woods alone; stay on the road.)

3. A little gardening every day. (We are here to care for the earth.)

4. Contact in person at least one other individual.

5. Do something for someone else who has a need—a letter, a phone call, a visit.

6. Do something creative—letter writing, keep a diary, paint, or write.

7. Do something about the arts, something with color and sound. Paint, or play an instrument or the record player. Not the radio; you must choose the music. (Color and sound work on you. We receive from color and the music we take in.)

8. Eat meals regularly, and cook three good ones a day.

9. Rest after lunch an hour or more.

10. Sit down and look at and appreciate beautiful things, paintings and sculptures in my art books. (In art forms man has transformed material things into spiritual.)

11. Take note of and sense the cosmic rhythm in nature, and ally yourself with this. (Have some time each day to get outside and experience this rhythm.)

12. Play music when getting a meal. Something rousing on the record player.

13. Plan ahead some special nice event for each day—a long-distance phone call, or something to anticipate all day.

14. Follow one whim every day—something nonsensical and fun.
15. Always have an interesting event in the future, the near future, and also the distant future. (A trip, a friend to come here to visit, a concert, a ballet, an all-day jaunt with a picnic, a painting expedition.)
16. Do a little something about business. (To learn gradually the things I need to know about.)
17. Do a little spiritual reading.

April 12
Today I suddenly remembered my book. About a month ago I settled by phone with my publisher and agent to do a book on wildflowers, and now the contract is due any day. How can I write this book, or any book now? I think it will be absolutely impossible. But on the other hand, how can I go back on my word? I have done quite a lot of thinking and planning for this book, and already have some notes down on paper. Bob and I had talked it over together before he went away. He always edited everything I wrote. How could I do it now without him? How could I do it anyway? I couldn't think straight about anything lately, least of all a book about wildflowers, much as I love them.

Should I write my agent and say I can't do the book?
No, I'll let it ride for the time being.

April 15
I was doing pretty well today until I went down to the cellar and caught sight of Bob's work bench and all his silver-making equipment and regular tools spread out. He was in the process of refinishing a little hand-carved

wooden mule made here in the mountains. He had stopped midway in sanding the little animal and left everything. Sandpaper and dust covered the bench. I really broke down then. The freezer is down there, and I will need to get things from it, so I will have to get used to this.

Bob and Tim took away all of Bob's clothes when they came, and I am glad they did. But I had been feeling that I had nothing left of his until I went down to the cellar and saw all his tools and equipment and the little partly sanded wooden mule. It was as if Bob had left the cellar a few minutes before.

April 17
We had known Betty and John since we moved here, and liked them so much. John died last week after a long illness in the hospital. I wrote Betty. What can I say to help another when I am so much in need of help myself? I know how she feels. Perhaps we can help each other if we can get together and talk things over. Unless you have lost someone near and dear you cannot know how it feels to be alone—that particular kind of aloneness. I went to see Betty today, and she was wonderful. We talked and spoke frankly about how we felt, and it did us both good.

I am thinking too much about myself lately, and now I can think of Betty and what I can do for her. We can share evenings together—evenings that will be as hard for her as they are for me.

We both cried a little when we got together today. Then, some way in our sharing, we sustained each other. Her family has been here until a day or so ago. She is experiencing that first terrible aloneness now, and I am remembering all too clearly how that is.

April 18

I have give-up moments and I have moving-ahead moments. In the midst of a give-up moment today out in the garden I saw a yellow butterfly. Is it a monarch? I looked it up. No, a swallowtail or milkweed butterfly. The monarch is the brown-orange one. Oh yes, I'll leave the butterfly book open here by the door to the terrace. We have a lot of different sorts these days, and it would be interesting to learn the varieties. And now I will be able to check when I see one.

So I got through another give-up moment, thanks to a yellow butterfly.

April 20

Out of the haze that had enveloped me since Bob died one person stands clearly—Jane. After the three children left, Jane came to the forefront, and has been there these weeks which have been so difficult. She is my Rock of Gibraltar, as Joan and Bob and Tim were at first. Jane, who leaves her night things here, saying, "I'll stay all night with you whenever you want me to. I can just as well sleep here as at home."

How many nights she stayed, and sat on the sofa in the living room before we went to bed while I poured out to her all that was on my mind and in my heart.

Jane, by her attitude, seemed to open a door, and I felt at ease and comfortable with her. I talked about Bob endlessly, and she listened. What a listener she turned out to be.

While Jane listened she never criticized, never told me what I ought to feel, think, or do—she just listened, and she *cared*.

It was Jane who brought two decks of cards, and we started playing double solitaire. I believe I laughed for the first time in one of our breathless games. It was Jane who called me every morning to see what kind of a night I had had. How welcome was the phone bell that rang so often during the day. Jane had found something in the paper she thought I would be interested in. There was a program on TV that night she thought I would like. There was a book she had read that might interest me. All this month, which has been such a difficult one, Jane was always there—at the other end of the phone when I called, and ready to come up at a moment's notice. I don't know whatever happened to her ordinary life and her customary day's events, but she made me feel that there was nothing I was interrupting, nothing she had to do more important than come up and stay with me a while, or sit and talk on the phone.

April 21
My contract for the wildflower book came in the mail today, and I realize if I sign it I am committed. I'm really committed anyhow. I agreed to do this book by phone and letter a couple of months ago. But can I follow through? Well, perhaps I can after all. There is a lot of research involved. Jane will type it for me. She is an expert typist. Maybe it will be somewhat steadying to have to look up and find out about a lot of wildflowers. Two hundred are involved.

I shall have to have some source material. Perhaps I'll

go over to the library one day soon and see if they have anything I can use. Meanwhile, I signed the contract and took it to the post office myself. Bob and I always had a kind of celebration when we signed a contract for the books we did together. We would go out to dinner or do something special. Today I signed this alone. I must get used to doing things alone now.

April 23
I cannot enjoy the garden or gardening as I used to. I feel nothing much as I work in the earth without Bob. We did a great deal in the garden together. This little vegetable plot was Bob's last gift to our outdoors, and I must keep faith with him by tending it well. Surely, sometime again I will feel the sense of well-being I always have had when I dig and plant and cultivate. I cannot have lost this forever. But when, oh when, will it return? This prolonged state of sadness I am in seems so all-enveloping.

Dr. Palmer says be patient with yourself. It is only three weeks and a little more. Don't expect to do much but hold where you are for a while.

April 24
Will I ever get used to being alone? I used to enjoy it. When Bob went to the Rotary or to the silver class I would settle on the terrace or in the living room and read, write letters, sew. I actually enjoyed the silence of the house and being by myself. Such a sense of peace I had, and contentment. But always there was the realization of our very pleasant reunion when Bob would come home with some interesting mail he had picked up at the post

office, some bits of news, a good idea he had thought of, or a plan to do something, drive somewhere.

Will I ever enjoy moments alone again? Will I ever find the same or a similar peace and contentment in solitude that I had all the years of our life together?

April 25
I have been trying to follow my list of ingredients of a day and have been partially successful, but it doesn't seem to make me feel any better. It does keep me going, and I guess that's good. I cook and eat three meals a day. This seems to me to be a must. It is not much fun planning meals for one or shopping for one. I keep buying too much of everything. The refrigerator is filled with food. Instead of buying two or three bananas I seem to get five or six. Then, of course, they don't keep. I have begun to ask a few close friends for dinner. My friends have been kind in asking me for lunch and dinner often, and I am returning the invitations now. Whenever we had company, Bob used to help me get dinner. It is very different now getting a company meal alone.

I am having a variety of problems. Things that are happening to me. One, my memory is getting very bad. I have heard of people who lose their minds as a result of an experience of grief. Will I lose mine? And if I should, what on earth will I do? Where can I go?

What happens is that someone tells me something, and then refers to what they have said, and I don't remember it at all. I guess I just didn't take it in in the first place. I still have the feeling I had so sharply those first few days after Bob died of being somewhere else, of not being present when I am speaking or listening, and hardly knowing what I have said or heard. I try hard to concentrate when someone is speaking to me and to listen. But mostly it is just impossible.

In the house here I am aware of Bob all the time. I imagine he comes in the room. I imagine I hear him moving around in another part of the house. Everything reminds me of him. I am having sort of a love-hate relationship with this place. I love it because we lived here together and had a wonderful few years. I hate it because I cannot seem to get away from heavy thoughts of grief and despair here in this house. I try to go somewhere every morning. I think up errands to do if I don't have any. When I do have some I spread them out so I will have an excuse to go tomorrow too. It helps to go somewhere—just anywhere. But when I get there I am in trouble because now, in the stores, all of a sudden I shrink from meeting people I know. I don't want to have to talk with them. The reason is that it is so difficult to take in what they say and to respond. However, I make myself talk and make contact with each other person, difficult as it is. This is one of my rules.

One reason why my memory is so poor is probably because my mind is divided. With about a quarter of it I am listening to my friends, and with the rest I am absorbed with Bob, thinking about him, remembering things we did together, remembering things he said at various times, imagining he is with me. I must try not to have my mind so divided.

I find it is getting more difficult now to go out to dinner with my friends. If it is a couple I am sharply and acutely aware of my loss. It is hard to be with people who are happily married.

I went to a concert the other night at the Art Center. When I got home and let myself in, the house was dark. It had been daylight when I left, and I hadn't thought to leave a light on. I came in the front door, turned on a light, and the most awful wave of loneliness swept over me. Was this how it would be the rest of my life—to come home alone and step into our living room where Bob and I had spent so many happy hours together—to know I would never be with him again in this room, this house, anywhere? This was more than I could take. I passed quickly through the living room; the bedroom and dressing room were even more lonely, and I got into bed as fast as I could. These days I dream a lot of Bob, and I hate to wake up in the morning to find myself alone. But it does make sleeping a joy. If I could only not wake up some day. I am just a trouble to my friends and family, and of no use to myself.

There is a large gap between wishing you were dead and dying, and I began to realize that all the wishing I would die that I might do had no effect whatever on the facts of the matter. So I was learning two things. Crying was useless, and so was wishing I would die.

April 26
I may as well accept the fact that I am alive and in the world. I need to make my peace with this fact. I need to see what there is constructive in my situation and initiate something useful and of a building nature. I have to find and begin a new life, a life alone, but one with a positive direction and a sense of purpose. I can't wait around for the larger purposes of my being alone to dawn on me. I will have to begin living with small purposes that I can

dream up for every day. Simple things I can do and work toward.

The first thing I can do is stop wishing I would die and learn to carry on one day at a time. The thing is I haven't much energy these days. I feel rather exhausted most of the time and don't do much. I am seventy-two years old, but surely I should have more energy than this.

When I go out shopping in the morning then I need to rest in the afternoon. I don't feel like doing anything else. When I have dinner company I don't plan anything else for that day.

April 27

Today I was watching a beautiful dragonfly with iridescent wings hover over the surface of our small pool, and nearby were a great number of large bumblebees humming among the blue steeples of ajuga. Can you look at any of nature's beauties without being aware of an underlying purpose? There is a rhythm in nature, and the seasons have direction and an existence with reason. Where there is rhythm there is plan and purpose. If there is purpose in nature there has to be purpose in our lives, too, and a reason and purpose in my being alone now, even if I cannot see it. I may never see why things are as they are, but if I can accept that there is some reason in all that happens and have faith and a knowing that this is so perhaps it will help. I wonder.

April 28

Bob's birthday.

Bob and I came down here as a couple. All our friends are couples, and now I feel incomplete and therefore strange when I go to a place where there are many couples. Something very peculiar has happened to me. A kind of silence has come over me when I go anywhere. I simply cannot say anything. Of course, I greet my friends when I first go in and answer questions that are asked me. But I cannot seem to initiate any conversation. There is some kind of a block there, and I seem unable to talk. I don't know what people think. I clearly have not one thing to say. I listen to conversations going on around me, but I cannot take in what is being said, nor can I participate. This is terribly rude. I find myself making excuses not to go when I am asked. This isn't good, to have come to dread going out.

I really think I am getting peculiar. Not only is my memory leaving me, and this losing the ability to talk, to exchange ideas, to communicate, but when people tell jokes and laugh, instead of joining in I feel like crying. Whatever is happening to me?

When I ask people to come to our house for dinner I cannot wait for them to go home. I just want to be alone. But when I am alone I am desperately unhappy. I don't make any sense.

Every Sunday night I telephone Joan. This is such a help. I can tell her just how I feel. I am learning that people don't want to be told anything unpleasant. When they ask how I am they want me to say that everything is fine. But I can be honest with Joan. And she helps me long-distance to see my way out of various hang-ups that occur.

April 30
Jane and I settled for our first morning on my book. My

method of working on a book is to do a lot of writing by hand, and then dictate it directly to the typewriter, changing it as I go along and see fit. I learned to do this years ago once when I had my right arm in a sling with tendonitis in my elbow, and I have done it ever since.

Much of the time I dictate straight from my head to the typewriter for a rough draft, and then work over this and make another draft.

When Jane came my mind was in such a swirl of thinking about Bob and I was feeling so miserable I didn't know if I could accomplish a thing. But at least I could try. Actually, it was good to have a focal point to concentrate on. It went far better than I thought. Maybe I can do this book after all.

May 10

Jane came over to see me, and we talked about Bob for about an hour. It was a great relief to be able to speak about him freely and at length. I long to talk about Bob, but everyone I see carefully avoids the subject. If I say anything about him, they usually quickly change the topic of conversation. I wonder why. They simply aren't comfortable discussing him. It is a relieving thing when I am able to casually refer to him. I can to Jane and to Joan.

I went to Dr. Palmer for some help, and he was wonderful. He began by giving me a vitamin B shot and says I am to have a series. He sat and talked with me for a long time, and I spoke freely of Bob. He says I have a lot of interests and a lot going for me and that I will be all right. I said my interests didn't seem to help me. His confidence in me, however, was very cheering.

Dr. Palmer explained that I was in a state of shock and

this was why I couldn't remember anything or really take in what was being said to me. The reason why I feel worse now than a few weeks ago, he says, is that I am emerging from a state of shock to a realization of what my loss really means.

What disturbs me most is the complete lack of reason for doing anything. I feel like a ship lacking a rudder, a boat adrift, blown by every wind that comes. I have no reason to get up in the morning. It was such a relief to be able to tell Dr. Palmer all this. He also reassures me that I am not losing my mind. He says being forgetful is a frequent reaction to the situation of grief and shock. I have such confidence in him I believe in him implicitly, and therefore feel much better.

"Even if you think you are losing your mind, and whenever you feel this way, tell yourself you are not and cannot," he said firmly.

I think I am really getting ready to believe there is a purpose in the universe and one in my life, even if I cannot see and understand it.

June 1
I always used to like the silence that comes from the absence of people and voices. The silence of a remote woodland, the quiet of being alone in a summer garden, or on a long stretch of sandy beach, or being in a house alone. All these and many more such experiences brought me a deep sense of peace and contentment. But now I don't like the silence in our house without another voice, or the awareness of movement of another individual.

I am lonely for the sound of someone speaking. I want

to hear another person stirring about. I feel no peace and contentment in the aloneness of this silence I am caught up in now.

June 10
I seem to be in a state of complete confusion today. I often get this way, and Bob always sorted me out. We would sit down and talk things over and settle on priorities and put first things first. Bob used to say, "Just think of one thing at a time, and go in just one direction until you become unconfused."

I try to imagine we are talking this over—this unhappy state I am in when I don't want to be alone and yet I don't want to be with people. I love this house, yet I hate it and want to be somewhere else, but don't know where.

Will I ever get out of this mire of grief? Will I ever have a reason to get up in the morning? I had been feeling so much better about everything, but now today I am sinking again. I wonder if I will ever feel again the sun on my back and arms when I am weeding in the garden with the sense of joy and fulfillment that I used to. The world is still a beautiful place. I have only to look out the window to see this. But when will I be able to *feel* it, be a part of it? When will I ever have again that delicious sense of peace and complete contentment that I so often used to feel in the garden, in the house, with people, or alone? Perhaps I will never get over this grief, but will merely learn to live with it, to accept it, to make friends with it. I wonder. I suspect there is no way out of this situation I am in, but only a way through it.

Meanwhile, I must go on living one day at a time. This I can cope with—not trying to think any further ahead than tonight. I make myself get up, make the bed (a few weeks ago I got lazy and didn't even make the bed half the time), straighten up the house, plan the meals. Then I refer to Joan's and my list of ingredients of a day. Am I having company? Or going out? I go out in the garden and do a little weeding and cultivate. I walk my mile. I work a couple of hours on the book. I contact another individual some time during the day, in the stores or at lunch at my house or going out to lunch. There is always someone in my life who needs something. I respond as well as I can with a phone call, a letter, a visit.

June 11

Friends can help, but I realize I have to do this alone—find my new path, and then learn to walk it by myself. I know in my mind that I can do this, but my emotions don't feel it yet. I alternate between despair and a sense of hope. At first I was numb. Now, an awful dawning of what has happened comes. The realization of just what has occurred comes home. The impact is terrible, and for a while I sink. Then again, there comes a slim newborn feeling of hope.

The world is still a beautiful place. I keep coming back to this. I know this with my mind, but I need to feel it, not merely know it. There is such a large gap between knowing and feeling. Can I ever close this gap? Will I ever feel one with the world's beauty again as I used to? I wonder.

I am in a situation I don't like at all. There is no way to step out of it now. The only out is the way through. I must go on, feeling as I feel, suffering through the different phases, living them, hopefully emerging eventually to find myself on a new path.

June 12

Recently I ran across some comments about grief by Elizabeth Gray Vining that I cherish.

> Grief is not something to overcome or to escape but to live with. It is always there, as perceptible as a person who will not go away in spite of hints or plain speaking, but one can make room for it, recognize it as a companion instead of an intruder, be aware of it but not possessed by it; one can continue one's work, one's occupations, even one's joys, in its presence.

I guess I have been possessed by grief.

Here is something else lovely that Mrs. Vining wrote that I can well take to heart.

> I shall no longer run from sorrow nor seek to avoid him
> by going down another street of thoughts.
> I shall not try to overcome him with my strength.
> I shall open the door of my heart to his knock and let him come in.
> Whether he be sorrow for my own loss or for the world's pain
> I will learn to live with him steadfast and tender.
> And some day the child, happiness, will play in the sunshine on the floor of my house.

June 16

Kay and Del are here, my sister-in-law and her husband—all the way from Cape Cod to spend five days with me. How truly wonderful of them.

I have a reason to get up in the morning now. Breakfast to get, and the challenge of making a different one each day. Baked eggs, griddle cakes, bacon and scrambled eggs, twelve-grain cereal. Del donned Bob's large apron and made delicious scrapple this morning, and he promises bran muffins for tomorrow. It is so wonderful to hear voices in the house. The great silence of these last two months or so has ended. I hear movement and conversation as they stir around in the Sunrise Room downstairs.

We drive up into the mountains and explore back roads. The Mimosa Inn pool is a joy to Kay and me. We swim every day. Del comes with us and watches. In the evenings we sit on the terrace and talk. I can speak as frankly as I want to these two dear people, and they are such a help to me, encouraging me and building my confidence in my ability to cope. When friends have confidence in me I gain confidence in myself. And when I have more self-confidence I have far fewer low moments. Kay and Del's visit is meaning a lot to me. I shall miss them when they leave.

June 20

The friends that help me the most are those who listen and care and who encourage me to talk, sometimes it is about Bob and how I am getting on, and sometimes other subjects.

Alas, I have some friends who begin with, "What is wrong with you, Jean, is . . ." or, "What you need to do is . . ." There is much wrong with me, I am sure, and I do not need or want to hear more in this vein. What I already know that is wrong undermines my confidence, and with no confidence I make no progress. Being told what is wrong undercuts my self-confidence still further, and leaves me feeling much worse.

Fortunately, I do not have very many friends who tell

me what is wrong, but I do have a few. I know they mean well, but they aren't very understanding, or really caring, or they would sense that their views of what I should do and how I should feel are not of any use to me at this point. I don't need things pointed out to me. Within me lie the answers and the direction markers. With the encouragement of a caring friend these come to the fore as my friend listens with love.

June 22
Today, in talking to a friend, I heard about a retirement center at Kennett Square, Pennsylvania, called Kendal. It is a collection of one-story buildings, each one a group of apartments. Every apartment has its own separate entrance. Large floor-to-ceiling glass doors open from the living room on to a terrace. The location is a rolling meadow surrounded by tall trees and woodlands. You can get one meal a day at the central dining room, or all three if you prefer. Your down payment and monthly rate cover lifetime medical care.

I wonder if this would be a place for me to move to. At the very thought of a move, something in me shrinks. When I came here to Tryon I said I would never move again. But I realize "never" is a long word, and not to be bandied about loosely. How could I ever leave this house, designed especially for us by our son Bob—the garden Bob Senior and I made and worked in together? How could I leave this place where we had been so happy? And yet there is this love-hate relationship between me and the house. At times I feel imprisoned in it, caught with memories of Bob and an awareness of how much I miss him. I am forever reminded of Bob here.

Can I possibly start a new life in Tryon where I am constantly caught up in the old ways?

At any rate, perhaps I should investigate this place. At least, I will write for more information.

July 1

Right after Bob died every person or acquaintance or friend went out of his or her way to be kind to me, to come over and talk to me at the Art Center events, in Cowan's market, in the bank, or on the street. Now I notice a subtle difference. People go on about their business. Except for a few close friends, the others just go on their own way, and don't bother much about me. I know just how this is, and why.

I have known a few friends who have lost a husband or wife. I have done things for them in the beginning, asked them for meals, and gone out of my way to speak to them. Then, after two or three months, I have decided that they were on their own feet now, and I have left them to their own devices. While this attitude of friends doesn't surprise me, it does create a kind of aloneness that I don't much relish. Especially because I find it so difficult these days to be outgoing, to project myself, to speak first to people. I find myself quite withdrawn, and try as I do I can't seem to help it. I draw into my own small world, lonely there, not wanting to be apart, yet being a person apart. I should try to be different, but it seems such an effort, and one I just can't seem to make.

July 6

I got a lot of literature from Kendal today describing the place and all the particulars. Jane is pretty interested in it too. We pored over it all evening. No solitaire tonight. We are both rather intrigued.

In a way, I feel a traitor to this house, to be considering leaving it. I am torn right in two by this drastic idea of a move to a retirement center. Jane and I discussed all the advantages and disadvantages.

We are not getting any younger. I don't want to be dependent on the children as I get older. I cannot go and live with any of them. Modern houses today aren't built for accommodating grandmothers as they used to be.

How can I leave here and sever my last link with Bob? Yet I am terribly unhappy here, terribly lonely. And in this community of couples do I, alone, have a place?

I have been feeling so peculiar physically lately—that lifetime medical care appeals to me.

At least I do think I should go up and visit the place. Maybe later on in the summer Jane and I might drive up. She is as interested in investigating Kendal as I am. It would be fine if she wanted to go too. Wouldn't it be great to be near Philadelphia and be able to attend the symphony regularly, and the ballet once in a while! That would be a real asset.

July 10

I was thinking about how it has been said, "Into each life some rain must fall."

Rain can be devastating, can flood, can destroy.

Rain also nourishes, causes seeds to sprout, feeds the roots of trees and bushes, brings growth and expansion to all that it reaches in the earth.

Can this experience of mine prove a source of growth and maturing instead of devastation and ruin?

July 14

I am discovering that, after all, crying does help. There seems to be a pattern in my times of weeping. Tension builds, and I get absentminded due to preoccupation. Then I have a good cry and talk to Jane about Bob. After this I notice my mind is clearer and stays focused better, and I have a sense of greater relaxation.

How can I ever repay Jane for all her listening? She says it is a growing experience for her, too.

I wonder.

July 15

Most of my friends have been quite wonderful to me ever since Bob died. But these days a few have begun to decide that by now I should be quite okay. "Never do anything for a person they can do for themselves lest you weaken them" is the attitude of certain people now that more than three months have passed. This is a harsh point of view and one that may apply in different circumstances, but definitely does not help the situation of grief.

If you have had a good marriage with a free interchange and a compatible interdependence as is true of most marriages that are basically good, there is a great need to have things done for you when you lose your partner. A great need to have someone you can depend on, a friend whom you can count on and lean on when you have a low moment. The cold attitude of the other way of thinking is like tossing you into a stormy sea on a winter night when you cannot swim. You are quite likely to sink. Right now I am and need to be dependent on another. I need the assurance that I can call, that my friend will help me by listening, by being there, by being my friend. Little by little, with this aid, I am beginning to find my own feet.

There is no human being who does not want to be on his own as much as possible. If he is dependent it is because he needs it at this point in the process of some adjustment. The worst slap in the face, the worst feeling of aloneness is thrust upon you by the attitude that, well, you are a big girl now and should be able to stand alone. If you cannot stand alone yet it is because you are absolutely unable to. The gradual and continual support of a friend is as vital as the air you breathe. To be deprived of this support will cause you to go under. But some people, alas, do not understand this. "For your own good." How many sins against another have been committed for their own good?

Certain people, fortunately only a few, seem to lose their common sense and basic kindliness—their humanness—in the face of a person in grief. They become filled with a harshness that is unbelievable. Not everyone, thank heaven, but enough people to upset you. In grief you are unusually sensitive and aware, and while they may not say they are doing this for your own good you feel them thinking it. The desertion and the rough approach causes a deep hurt that is a long time healing. And you feel no need at all for that person's company.

There is no joy keener than, after a great loss, coming upon, in your own way, at your own time, the first slight hint of a sense of independence. This begins to grow within you as a small frail plant. It needs the most loving care and nurturing.

At the first sign of the way of thinking of "let her be on her own now, she is adult," and "it has been long enough we have considered her," the tender young plant shrivels and dies, and one must begin all over.

It is the same principle as the fact that any ideas or attitudes of change that come to you from within are worth twenty times those that someone else presses upon you in the way of advice.

In a grief situation we seldom grow from advice, but from our own insights. From being loved and listened to, and cared for. This brings out our abilities to stand alone, and is the only thing that does. Will well-meaning friends ever learn this? I doubt it. One has to give them A for effort, they mean to be kind and helpful, but a flat failure of E for performance—if their desire is to help the person who is in grief.

July 17
Friends who live on a lake in New Jersey invited me for a week's visit. I had some hesitation, feeling I didn't have the energy to make the plane trip. But finally I decided to come. So here I am, installed in the guest room, looking out over the lake. It really did something good to my confidence to find I could negotiate the plane trip.

I left my book at a good stopping place at home. It is pleasant to have a little recess from it. I have been quite deep in it for some weeks now.

July 24
I observe that when I am away from home I don't think about Bob so much. Perhaps I shouldn't say I don't *think* about Bob, but my thinking about him is different. I think of him with appreciation for what our life together meant. I am not so obsessed with missing him. I am not

so miserably lonely. It is easier to follow what other people say, to participate in conversations with others. I seem to feel better generally when I am away from home. At home, I miss Bob terribly. As the months go by, this doesn't seem to get better, but worse, if anything. I believe I surely will have to look into Kendal, the retirement center.

July 26
In all our married life Bob and I had never discussed what we would do if one of us died first. We never thought about death or dying. We never thought about one of us being alone. I wish we had, and had talked over death and what the one left might do. I never thought Bob would die before I did. My parents lived to their nineties. Bob was so healthy and well I thought we would have at least another ten years together. I imagined we would live on here gently growing older together, but always having each other. I pictured our enjoying each other, our friends, and our families for many more years. I assumed this was how it would be.

I believe that, as we get older, we should all of us discuss death and what would happen to the one left. I wish I had asked Bob to explain to me some of the business end of things. I am so at sea now in this area.

August 1
Jane and I are going up to Kendal, which is thirty miles south of Philadelphia. We have made appointments for interviews.

August 3

We arrived yesterday. Kendal is most attractive. Individual apartments each have a terrace and a garden. There are many advantages to living here. We are staying in the Farm House, a place for visitors.

Mr. Lewis, the director, explained that Kendal was full, with a long waiting list, but they are building a new and similar adjoining unit called Crosslands, to be ready in September 1977. Jane and I decided to sign up. We could think it over for the next two years. You can withdraw any time should you want to.

Now and then, as we wandered around and explored the place on our own, I would have a terrible pang to think of leaving our house, the brook, the wooded hillside, my garden, my beloved kitchen, and the bedroom where I went to sleep listening to the brook.

But there was always the refrain in my mind.

"You are not getting any younger. You will need to be somewhere as you get older. Why not move before you have to, get settled in while you still have the energy to make friends, to explore your new territory, and to enjoy the cultural happenings of Philadelphia? Why wait until you are decrepit to move to a retirement center?" So went the mental struggle, to move or not to move.

August 15

There is such a large gap between my mind and my emotions.

I can reason it out perfectly well, this whole situation I am in. My mind tells me that we had fifty years of a wonderful marriage. That Bob's time to go had come. That he was lucky to go the way he did, without a long illness. Drawing on the richness of our life together those many years, I should have ample resources and strength to start anew. I am fortunate that this didn't happen ten years ago or longer. How glad I am that we had these years of retirement together. We did have an idyllic retirement that was a mixture of wonderful trips and delightful months of staying home. It is nearly impossible for two people, no matter how close they are and how much they love each other, to die at the same moment. One has to go first.

I am willing to accept what has happened to me as being part of a larger plan, and I can assent to there being a reason for all that occurs to us. I guess the right thing happened.

All these things my *mind* accepts and believes.

But my emotions are way out in left field. They are telling me that there is nothing lucky about any of this, and nothing good about it. That it is all pretty awful, and living is not a happy experience for me without Bob.

How can I get my mind and emotions to merge and agree?

August 20
Here it is five months since Bob died, and I should be feeling much more balanced and have more direction than I have. At least, according to what I read between the lines of what most of my friends say. I sense they feel that my period of difficulties should be entirely over and I should be cheerful and happy and quite as before. They don't tell me this in so many words, but they hint at it. I hate to let them down. Yet I feel a lot worse. It is as if each week I realize more clearly what I have lost.

I am beginning to realize that I will never again be as before. I don't think that I will ever again be cheerful and happy in the ways I was before Bob died. I am sure I will be cheerful and happy some time, and I hope before too long, but it will be different. Everything is and will be different.

Dr. Palmer keeps on saying, "Don't be hard on yourself. Don't make yourself act better than you feel to fool yourself. Fool your friends by a little acting if you must. Sometimes this is expedient. But never fool yourself. Be where you are. Have a good cry when you feel like it, and admit to yourself when you hit bottom. From the bottom the only way is up."

Dr. Palmer thus shares his wisdom with me. He explained one day recently that I am now getting the true impact of my loss, and that is why lately I feel so much worse.

August 25

A large heaviness seems to have settled in somewhere between my heart and my stomach. It is ever present. I talk and I laugh; I write my book; but then in the interludes, the silence that comes, I lapse into an awareness of this weight that never leaves me day or night. Will I always have this? This goes with the kind of inner quivering that I feel so often these days.

September 1

Over the years, from time to time, I have been given sleeping pills to take. I've never taken them very long, and have saved the remainders. I must have an awful lot left in the house. If I took enough of them that would be

the end of my struggle here alone. That would end my
battles with the illnesses I have had since early summer
and the difficulties of adjusting to life alone. I have had a
lot of illnesses since Bob died.

But there is something in me that won't take this way
out.

I really do believe that there is some purpose in my
life, and a reason why I am here.

No, that door is one I will not walk through, no matter
what. Other ways must evolve, and I guess I am the one
to evolve them. And this is positively the last time I will
entertain any thoughts about taking my life. Or even
wishing I would die.

September 5

When I wasn't consistently cheerful and gay after three
or four months I began to feel guilty and as if I were
letting my friends down. They appear to think all is well,
and I wish it were. Actually, as I look back now, six
months later, I realize that I am only just coming out of
my coma, and the full impact of what has happened is
still hitting me. I am feeling in some ways far worse than
I did at first. It has been a lifesaver working on my book,
which is nearly finished now. While I am concentrating
and dictating to Jane, I am less aware of the heaviness in
my solar plexus—less aware of the inner quivering. I get
so wrapped up in the book I am totally with it almost to
the exclusion of all else.

October 16

Some days are already made when you awaken. The air
sparkles, the sun streams down, bringing life and vitality

to all on earth. You get filled with direction and purpose. You have energy and desire to see everything you touch through to the end.

Other days you have to make something of yourself. You waken to grayness and rain—a kind of beneficent rain such as the earth frequently needs for a day or so, but nonetheless a steady downpour. No direction occurs to you as you eat breakfast, and no purposes seem very important. This day you must take hold of and mold it into shape, give it direction and reason to be.

Such days, after we have made them into something, can be the most satisfying of all. After we have shaped them and gone through them, they help shape us, help form the pattern of what we are.

October 18

Bob did management counseling work for a number of years, and recently I came across an interesting chart in his study.

Dr. Thomas Holmes, professor of psychiatry at the University of Washington, and Dr. Richard Rahe, of the U. S. Navy Medical Neuropsychiatric Unit in San Diego, devised this chart. Holmes and Rahe and their associates, after years of research involving thousands of interviews with patients, came up with a test called "A Social Readjustment Rating Scale." It indicates what the chances are of your becoming ill within the next year or so. If your score is above 150, you have a fifty-fifty chance of being ill. If your score is 300 or above, you have an 80 percent chance of sickness being in your immediate offing.

Topping the list of life events is the death of a spouse,

with a point value of 100. Other life events include business readjustment, with 39 points; change of residence, 20 points; death of a close friend, 37 points; etc. But heading the list is the death of a spouse.

Dr. Palmer says that the basic cause of my illnesses and ailments is the situation of living through the loss of my husband and adjusting to new ways and a different pattern. In looking over the stress-causing life events list, my score was well over 200, so no wonder I have had problems.

October 20
Betty came down the mountain to have dinner with me. Betty, whose husband died a few weeks after Bob. We do each other so much good. We have eaten many meals together during the summer, and are a great help to each other. It is a relief when I feel some peculiar way and find she does too. Then we both laugh and decide that this is just par for the course. I think she is ahead of me in lots of ways. She is more comfortable going out in groups of people. Betty says it is hard, but she goes anyway. She never did have the block I have had about not being able to talk and initiate any conversation when I go out. Thank goodness, I am getting over this now.

October 22
This is a gala day to celebrate. I finished my book. Went to the post office to mail it this morning. I felt so good. It has been a satisfying experience to be able to do it at this time. As a matter of fact, my contract gave me until next spring, and it is rather exciting to have finished so far ahead of schedule.

I shall miss this book. But I received a letter from my agent recently saying that the publisher wants another one on annuals and perennials after I have had a little interlude. This will be interesting to do, and helpful to me, I am sure. It is great to have a focal point. I can start rounding up books for my research. Most of the varieties I will use I have grown myself, so have personal experiences to draw from. Well, I guess I won't begin thinking about this next book immediately, but will pause to enjoy the completion of the wildflower one.

November 2

Bob and Tim and Joan came to visit me. They overlapped a bit, so one or another of them was here for a week, and the last one left today. This was a great experience. They had said when they were here in the spring that they would return in six months to see how I was getting along, and this is what they did. It was just wonderful to have them here, all three. Bob and Tim went over Bob Senior's files and helped me get rid of a lot of file folders that I needn't keep.

We sorted and threw away countless old letters and photos. They helped me with some business matters. It was a wonderfully productive week, with major and minor decisions made and numerous business details that had been dangling tied up and settled.

I told them about my visit to Kendal, and we discussed the pros and cons. We also discussed the possibility of my moving west to a retirement community that was part way between Sacramento and San Francisco. There I would be near both Bob and Tim. I guess I should consider both locations.

November 20

The new book has gone well these last two weeks since I started it. I have to do long captions for a hundred annuals and a hundred perennials. I have started with the annuals. We grew so many of these glorious flowers in Connecticut before we moved down here. I remember them all. Their needs and traits are fresh in my mind, as is our whole Connecticut garden.

Here we have a much smaller garden, equally loved and more appropriate for us at this time of our lives. There is no grass at all to mow. No beds for annuals. Very few perennials. Some chrysanthemums are blooming now—late ones—and the leaves are falling more every day. Autumn in the mountains is a rich, rewarding time of year. The air is so crisp and fresh.

Bob used to love the fall. This was the season we took long walks and explored new mountain trails. I don't walk so much any more. I go around the circle from our house here, which is one mile. I try to do this every day. Jane often comes up and goes around it with me. Or I go with Amy, who lives at the other side of the circle. Or I go alone, which isn't nearly as much fun.

November 30

I went to some friends' house for Thanksgiving dinner. Bless them for asking me. Holidays are difficult times just now. Bob and I always did something special. On these days I miss him a great deal. We had dinner at six. Afterward we sat and talked beside their fire. The evening was a warm and friendly one, and I didn't like to leave.

I never enjoy coming home to my dark and lonely

house. I often forget to put a light on when I go out in the evening.

I have been thinking more about Crosslands lately. I seem to favor it over the retirement center in the west. I guess that's because I have seen the adjoining center at Kendal and liked it so much. I wonder if I would enjoy living there. Jane is all for it. She thinks it is a great idea for us to go. I wish I had her certainty. I am of two minds about it. One day, yes, the next, no. What would Bob have thought of it, I often wonder. How I wish we had discussed what we would do if one of us went before the other. Why did it never occur to me that this could happen? Other people lost husbands. I knew several who had. But this would never happen to me, was my attitude whenever I thought about it, which was seldom.

December 5

This is our anniversary. We would have been married fifty years today. How well I remember our wedding day. It was misty and rainy. The wedding took place in the living room of my sister's home.

"I, Robert, take thee, Jean . . ." I can hear Bob's voice now. This part of the ceremony, usually repeated after the minister, phrase by phrase, we had learned by heart. And we each said our part without error. We had been practicing it for weeks. When we got to the hotel in New York City where we were to spend our first night together, Bob took off his hat at the desk to register, and some confetti fell out of his hair onto the counter. The clerk smiled.

"Been in a storm, sir?" he asked.

Jane came up for dinner, and afterward we sat in the

living room by a cozy fire and talked and talked. I was feeling rather downhearted, and felt like talking about Bob, and it certainly did me a lot of good. Jane gets A as a listener. I never knew a better one. After she left I went to bed fast so I wouldn't do too much thinking. But talking out my low spirits with Jane had been wonderful therapy.

December 10

Joan will be here in another ten days and will stay a week. Jeffrey, her youngest son, age twenty-three, will be here too.

I fear this first Christmas after Bob has died may be a little difficult. But if I put my mind for all it's worth on Joan and Jeffrey and giving them a good holiday, this should help.

Bob and I always decorated the house together, and each year he put a little pine tree out on the terrace and strung lights on it. Only lights, nothing else. We had some very tiny twinkling bulbs that were magical. But this year perhaps we won't have the tree on the terrace. I don't believe I could put it up myself. We shall be as merry as we can with our decorations indoors and our candles at the windows.

December 24

Joan, Jeffrey and I had a wonderful evening together. We lit all our candles, pulled the curtains to make it cozy, and built a fire. We played Christmas carols on our recorders, Joan and I doing duets while Jeffrey sang. All our old favorites. "Noel," "Hark, the Herald Angels Sing," and "Oh, Little Town of Bethlehem." I believe that is the one I like best of all. No, I also love "What Child is This?" the one to the tune of "Greensleeves." I guess I love them all.

Last year we had been a trio with recorders. Bob played the soprano, Joan the alto, and I the tenor, while Jeff was singing. We all spoke of the previous year and of Bob, and some way we almost felt him there with us.

Later, there was a flurry and rustle of tissue paper and the usual air of mystery and secrets as we wrapped last-minute presents and arranged them under the little Mexican tree with its glowing white candles.

We all went to bed about ten. It had been one of those wonderful and warm family evenings. We were all thinking of each other and trying to make it easy for the other person, succeeding to a degree. It was great to be all together and to sense Bob's presence with us. I thought of the sound of his voice, his wonderful laugh, his enthusiasm and interest in everything, and his voice singing carols. Some of the carols we played on the recorder always, and some we sang. Bob had a fine singing voice. Jeff's voice is good too.

December 31
Jeffrey left yesterday. I had a good cry last night, but it didn't do me much good. Being all alone on New Year's Eve made me feel rather desolate. But I told myself sternly that I had ten days of beautiful memories stored up, and remembered all the pleasant things we had done, so I should cheer up. I finally did, and went to sleep in a very quiet house—much too quiet.

The holidays are over, and I realize Joan and Jeffrey had saved them for me by their love and concern and good spirits. It is peculiar, when you think of it, that we should be mournful when someone we love has left this life. Bob would not have wanted me to be sad. He would have wanted me to carry on. This is about it. We have to do our best to keep going. In so doing, time passes, and my spirits gradually and slowly lift a little more each week—with, of course, now and again a good dip or a backward slip.

The Second Year

January 2

I got back to my annuals and perennials book this morning. I had stopped working on it over the holidays. It is good to again have a focal point, and the book progresses. Some mornings I don't want to get up at all. I have no desire to face the day and do the things I must do. But I make myself. So much of living these days is pushing myself in some direction or another. I seem to have no inward urge, no natural excitement about what the day will offer, no eagerness to get up and into it. I suppose this all will return to me in due time. I hope so. To live on from day to day with no spark of real interest and excitement about doing anything would be difficult.

Having a book to write is a big help. I am committed to do it, and must just put one foot before the other and go on with it each day. The weather is cold, so I settle snug and comfortable in the living room with all my source material, pencils, and yellow paper and get on with it.

January 5

I ran an ad a few days ago for my creative-writing class. I have done this for two years now, and I love it. I do six sessions, and have eight people in the class. The idea is not learning to write for publication, but writing as a means of self-expression. The joy of writing letters, keeping a diary, just writing. Write out your joys and they double, once in living them, once in recapturing them and getting them down on paper. Write out your heartaches and they halve. When you get them down on paper and out of your system you see them objectively and with a little perspective, and they don't seem so terribly important in the general overall scheme of your life. Often, in getting down on paper some difficult or puzzling situation, you begin to see what you can do next and how to surmount it. My writing class is a little different from most. And I love doing it. I already have my eight people, and am establishing a waiting list in case some drop out before I start the class. This sometimes happens. I have four from last year and four new ones.

This is how I first met Jane. She answered an ad for my first year of creative writing. She was in the class, and we began to be friends then.

I give the class homework, and we read it aloud and discuss what each piece lacks and what is good about it. I like to see a group learn to criticize another's writing.

I find my writing class is like planting a garden. I have the pure joy of seeing each one improve each week. This is fascinating. It is like sowing a seed, waiting for it to come up, watering and cultivating it, and watching it grow. It is a little different every day. So with my pupils in writing. Each week their work changes and they become better.

I give them subjects every lesson to take home and do, such as: The Most Moving Experience of the Week; My Favorite Time of Day and Why; An Imaginary Conversation with an Animal; My Favorite Room in the House of My Childhood; My Earliest Memory as a Child. When the class has progressed a bit, toward the end, I ask them to carry on a conversation with a tree. Stand beside a brook and feel one with it. Write what you feel.

The last time I had them imagine they were in the picture on our wall of Rousseau's *Sleeping Gypsy*, and write what happens there.

You can see what a good time I have and how exciting it is from week to week to see what each one comes up with. It is so rewarding to follow a group of people whose imaginations are stirred and wakened.

I am looking forward to my class, starting in two weeks.

January 22
The new class gathered this morning at ten o'clock. What a good morning it was. Brilliant sunshine, very auspicious. I start off each time with a short talk on some one point to concentrate on in the assignment, such as verbs that are alive and expressive. And, of course, in the first lesson I explain the purposes and general direction of the course. I have an interesting group. Some will be so good. I can hardly wait for the second session to see what they write. That was the way I felt this morning.

Now this evening, I have a different reaction. I feel just exhausted and have a terrible headache. Oh dear, I do love teaching writing, and hope I can do this class. I wonder if it is too soon to start something like this?

January 23
I have to admit that I fear it is too soon for me to be doing a writing class. I did feel so tired last night, and now the thought of next week and having the group again is some-

thing I cannot face. It was exciting to do the class when Bob was living. I always talked it all over with him after each session. Often I would read him the papers as I worked over them. He was a wonderful editor and frequently came up with some fine suggestions. I guess I was missing his company after my first class. It seemed to throw into relief how much I miss him in general. Can I do nothing without him? Well, I can write my book. I am deep in the annuals and perennials now. I guess it will be better if I stay with that and not try anything else extraneous. But what a disappointment to me.

I had such a good group, and I had so liked the previous years. I guess I have to accept the fact that there is a time for everything, and this is not the moment for me to do a writing class. I called each person up and explained that I couldn't continue.

February 20
I have finished the chapters and captions of annuals now and will soon start on perennials. The book is half done.

Our daffodils are coming out. The tiny short-stemmed ones that Homer gave me by the dozen a couple of years ago. The crocuses have come and gone. The daphne *odora* is in flower now and so fragrant that I smell it the minute I open the front door to go out. Bob always liked the first signs of spring. Together we appreciated how different the birds sound as spring approaches. Their tones seem richer and more mellow. Hard to describe, but you notice a difference. And now, in the marshes, the first peepers are beginning to chant their nightly serenade.

The turns of the year, the beginnings of a new season, are always so exciting. How willingly we loose and let go of winter as spring starts. Can we always let go of the season we are leaving behind? Can we as readily let go of a certain period of our lives when we enter a new phase? This is what I have to work with now, letting go of the part of my life when I was married. Not that I have to obliterate it. I guess I couldn't do this anyway. But I have to slip out of it, stop clinging to the way things were. I have somehow to translate my thoughts about my life with Bob to a pleasant memory, not an agonizing longing. Sometimes I can do this; other times I cannot. When I stop and reason it out, I am able to draw a kind of strength from having been married to Bob for fifty years. But sometimes I cannot do this. I can only think back with longing. I am unable to loose those fifty years and start a new tune, as the birds do in spring.

Perhaps this will be different if I move to Crosslands. In a new environment, can I more easily face and begin a new life? Maybe so. These days I am of two minds about Crosslands. (1) I enjoy my house here and want to remain in it, but (2) I will be glad to try a new environment and see if I can more readily loose and let go of the past and begin a new phase of living in Crosslands.

Sunday, when I talked to Joan—I still call her each week and have a wonderful conversation with her—she and I discussed my possible move too, and she thinks it would be a good thing to do. I said I didn't see how I could ever make the actual move. It would be such a vast project and take so much energy. She said she would come and stay a few days and help me. I have had recent letters from Bob and Tim, who say that if I decide to go they will each come and stay a week at the time of my leaving here and help. This will be a lifesaver. Maybe, with all this aid from the children, I will be able to negotiate one more change at this time of life. I wonder.

March 11
Mostly, these past months, when I thought of Bob, I did so with an all-pervading ache of loneliness, with a sense of irreparable loss, and with a deeply depressed feeling. But now something new has been added. There is a change of emphasis. There is the engulfing aloneness, yes, but there is a constructive note that just lately begins to creep into my thoughts. And I think of Bob often. Lately, I do so realizing what a good background of our years together I have to draw on for this new chapter of life alone. I think of this with more peace and contentment—aware that I have a lot going for me to start. A great deal of past joy and many enriching experiences lie behind me. All of which provide ample material for sustaining me on this new path that I must walk alone.

April 26
I went to Kendal to have my entry interview for Crosslands. While there I learned you could rent an apartment at Kendal during the summer when the owner was away. If I did this for a month this summer I would get a feel of how it would really be to live in a retirement center. This would be a good idea, I decided. I'd give it a try for five weeks in August. I had visits to pay in July, so I'd do them first.

May 5

I got a note confirming my choice of apartments at Cross-lands. Mine is on the ground floor of a two-story building. It has a southern exposure and a lovely terrace off the living room.

May 15

I have packed a bag, and Jane will soon take me to the hospital. Dr. Palmer thought I should go. I've been struggling with labyrinthitis coming and going for the last five weeks. Before that, and ever since Bob died, I have been having a series of ailments—bursitis, cystitis, gastritis—and now this persistent dizziness.

I am so depressed because I have the feeling I will never get well in the hospital. I am in a real panic about being there. This is the first time I have been really sick and needing a hospital without Bob. He was so wonderful and steadying whenever I got sick. And when I had to go to the hospital he was always there helping to lift my spirits.

May 20

I needn't have panicked so much about the hospital. Dr. Palmer said just to give over and let myself be ministered to. This I am glad to do. Meals come, nurses and doctors walk in and out and write things on charts, and all the while the room gently swirls.

Dr. Palmer says just relax, and don't think of going home. I read and sleep and don't even think. The color scheme of the pills changes from time to time. Every day I am a little less dizzy. It is a wonderful thing to have the world grow gradually steady.

May 25

Bob and Tim call me every few days. Joan calls, and Jane comes.

How much good it does us once in a while to give over the responsibility for our lives and just go on day after day with no plan and no goals. I just eat and sleep and bathe, and in this lovely weather I have special permission to go and sit out in the patio in the sun and enjoy spring. My dizziness is almost gone—only when I sit up suddenly or when I bend over do I notice it.

May 26

I am to go home in a few minutes. It has been a most successful stay here, and I feel much better. I have enjoyed having a visit and talk with Dr. Palmer every day. He is so calm and reassuring. The nurses have been kind and helpful, and my friends have been wonderful. They have brought me flowers and books and good things to eat.

Jane is going to stay at my house nights for a couple of weeks. The doctor asked her if she would and urged her to stay even if I assured her I didn't need her.

July 14

Last week I took the plane heading north to visit in Connecticut, where we used to live before we moved to Tryon. I am staying with an old friend and neighbor. Yesterday, after an early supper, we drove up to our old house. There was no one home. We parked the car and walked around the building, peering in the windows. What an experience. Our little greenhouse, where we grew orchids, is converted to a breakfast room. The interior color scheme is all different, and the furniture, of course. Our wild meadow, where we had thousands of daffodils and summer daisies and black-eyed susans is now a swimming pool and mowed lawn. It was our house and it wasn't. A strange feeling it all gave me. I was looking at the lawn where some asparagus spears were coming up and feathering out, and I wasn't seeing it like that at all. But rather, our large and productive vegetable garden, with Bob and me working there together. In July we would have been harvesting our peas and spinach, tying up tomato plants, mulching the asparagus. And now we walked over and under the grape arbor, Janet and I, and saw the great bunches of green grapes hanging from the trellis. I am remembering Bob and me pruning these same grapevines and standing there on mellow September days when they ripened, eating and eating, and always the sound of the brook. Bob and I were wading there, setting out watercress in the shallows, and there in the deep shadows upstream were three trout wavering in the water. Now it was a summer evening, and Bob and I were lying in the hammock by the brook listening to the occasional frog and the splash as it dove out of sight. The stars were out and tangling in the maple branches overhead.

No—no—no—that was then, and this is now. I must not be captured by what was, but must remain in the now. It is today, and Janet and I are wandering over our old place, trespassing (I always did like to trespass), and there are a few mosquitoes here by the brook. We must go up to the house, I thought, and get in our car and go back to Janet's. There, we sat on her porch and talked a bit, and then we went to bed—me to my lonely bed in the guest room, with my memories all fresh and alive, and no sleep for a while.

August 10
Now I have been at Kendal for a week. I delight in my cozy small apartment. People are very friendly and warm. There are 250 apartments here, and each one with its own terrace garden. Every garden is different from the next one. Here is a spot that is masses of flowers like an English garden. Here is a little pool with a water lily, some water-lily pads, and enchanting water bugs. Over beyond is a shady garden with ferns and mosses and shade-loving plants. I like to walk around after supper and see all the different gardens and converse a little with the owners working there—pulling a weed, transplanting, tying up.

August 20
People here are so interesting. I had trouble with names at first, but I got a little notebook and wrote down all new names as I encountered them, and something special about each person. This is a great help. People do appreciate it when you remember the name and call them by it.

I am liking everything about Kendal enormously, and am feeling that perhaps the new unit, Crosslands, is really the place for me. Crosslands is under construction now. It is very like Kendal, and will be ready in September 1977. All people recently on the waiting list will go into that. The new buildings are on an equally lovely piece of land that adjoins Kendal. They broke ground some weeks ago for Crosslands, and each week there is much progress to be seen.

Something bothered me a great deal here at first. In fact, for a few days I thought I couldn't live here because of it. There are a number of people around who are handicapped in some way—lame, on crutches, or rather ill in one way or another. This seemed to me to be very depressing. But no, I found that as I got to know some of these particular people I began to admire them for their courage and stamina, and I ceased to be aware of their handicaps. I stopped feeling sorry for them.

Now it doesn't bother me one bit to see someone rolling along in an electric cart. There are several of these here. They are lifesavers for those who need them.

Yes, I believe I will enjoy living at Crosslands. It is valuable to be here sampling this kind of living, because I am getting a clear sense of just how it will be.

One interesting thing has happened here. I have a sense of being invited to go for dinner or lunch because I am me. I have felt this last year and a half since Bob died that so often I am asked places because of him or because someone feels sorry for me.

Here at Kendal no one has any reason to ask me anywhere, and so when they do it is because they really want me. This is a good feeling. I am beginning to discover me again, and to feel like myself. It is as if I am finding myself again after a long gap when I was lost to myself.

I haven't felt that the person I have been this last year and a half is really me. The ways I have felt are new and unfamiliar. I have been sick and ailing so much. I haven't cared, really cared, to go anywhere, and I seem to have developed a lot of queer traits. I hope these aren't me. I would hate to think the real me is like that.

September 2
What a rich month I have had here at Kendal. In a few days now I shall go home to Tryon, after being away two months. I feel so much better physically than when I came a few weeks ago. I have a great deal more energy. I think about Bob a lot, but it is an appreciative kind of thinking. I am aware of how lucky I am to have had the long, rich period of fifty years together. We did so much, and in our last years together we traveled a lot. We explored Greece, England, Switzerland, Germany, France, and Italy. We drove through all these countries and had a series of unique and marvelous holidays together. Every summer we would go for at least two months.

If I don't travel extensively anymore I will have the sense that I have already done so. I am toying with the idea now of taking a cruise to California via the Panama Canal and visiting the two families out there. I really think this would be a wonderful idea for this fall. It is easy and not long. I feel so much better physically I believe I could do it. Jane sent me an ad of the Royal Viking Line Caribbean cruises. I sent for some literature, and it looks tempting. I think I should try going alone. I have written Bob and Tim to see if October would be a good time to visit them—late October.

Now when I go home I will need to start in sorting and clearing out the house. I will have to give a lot of thought to reducing my belongings so they will fit into a one-bedroom apartment instead of a six-room house. It has been helpful living in that size apartment this summer. I find it very cozy and not cramped a bit. I believe my weeks here this summer have converted me to Crosslands. I shall give up the idea of the retirement center in the west. I shall give up the idea of staying on in the Tryon house. In many ways this latter will be difficult.

It is so funny how Betty still loves living in the house where she and John shared their many years of retirement together. I suppose we are all different. While I find it difficult to live in my house in Tryon, she would feel lost out of hers. She feels she can best start her new life right there where she is. I am constantly missing Bob in Tryon, whereas here at Kendal all month, while I miss him and think a lot about him, it is a different kind of missing. I feel proud to remember the life I have led. I am able to draw from it for enrichment. Draw strength and encouragement from what has been. In Tryon I am all mixed up between what is and what has been. What *is* is in the middle of what has been, and at times drowns in it. I am too close to gain any perspective.

September 16
I am so happy to be feeling better physically. I also feel my initiative returning. I find I care about going places now, and am ready and interested to meet people. I am enjoying encountering friends on the street and stopping to chat with them instead of finding this a burden and something to shrink from.

September 29
My birthday. My second birthday since Bob died. Jane and I had dinner together at our house. We took a walk first around the double circle. This is two miles, not one,

and an attractive walk. We sat in the living room after dinner and talked and had our first small fire. I have had so much to catch Jane up with about my summer. I got calls from all three children, which were lovely. It is always so great talking to them.

Next week I shall be leaving.

October 6

I flew to Port Everglades and there boarded a Royal Viking Line ship.

It feels funny to be on a ship without Bob. He was very fond of going places by sea, and I equally so. And we went to Europe many times that way. But now it is all different. I am alone. The people are friendly, but few seem to be by themselves. Mostly there are couples or groups. I wonder how I shall like this being by myself.

We had interesting stops at St. Thomas, Caracas, La Guaira. The Panama Canal and Mexico are ahead of us.

October 22

There is an easy pleasant rhythm to these days at sea— walking around the deck, swimming, reading, talking to the person in the next deck chair. I love to just look out at the horizon and the blue, blue water. You never know when you will see a school of flying fish, a porpoise or two, or a whale spouting.

October 23

Tomorrow we dock in San Francisco, and I shall be glad. If only I had had a friend with me I would have liked the cruise better. It was lonely. I kept being reminded of ships Bob and I had been on together. We used to sit up on the upper deck in the moonlight listening to the waves against the ship. On this ship there was dancing every night after supper. Bob danced so well, and we enjoyed waltzing together. I will remember not to take another cruise alone.

October 26
How wonderful it is to be with my family, Bob and Susan, and their two boys, Miles, 14, and Galen, 9. Miles is as tall as his father. I hadn't seen them for four years. They all seemed pleased with the presents I'd brought them from Mexico.

Last night we went on a picnic to one of the nearby beaches. We cooked dinner over a fire and walked along the shore in the moonlight, our shoes kicking up phosphorus in the wet sand. The sea air was so fresh and invigorating. The fire on the beach sent up sparks and the wind blew them swirling high above.

October 29
Susan and I have been painting together, tugboats in the harbor one day, and mountains rising out of the sea another. We've been to exhibitions. We've had wonderful conversations in the evenings, we three adults. I have promised to make Miles a new patchwork quilt to replace the worn-out one I made him years ago. And now Galen wants one also.

November 3
I moved from San Francisco to Sacramento to visit Tim and Jeanne and their two, Mandy and Timmy, 16 and 14. After a few days there, having a wonderful warm

family time and getting reacquainted with the grandchildren, exploring their area, meeting the neighbors, and appreciating their garden, I flew home.

Now I have had my fling—two flings, Kendal and the west. I must settle down and begin working on the house. In less than a year I will be moving, and there is so much I must clear out and sort over and discard. As soon as I am unpacked and settled in I will begin, and no more travels for a while. But it was all more than worthwhile. It did so much for me, this trip, the cruise, and then the California visit, and the plane trip home. It proved to me that I can do things like this now alone. I know this sounds foolish. But I had never traveled anywhere without Bob for many, many years. Being sick a lot robs you of confidence. It is hard to have much assurance about your body when it has done as many queer things as mine has since Bob died. But now I do feel quite different. Since my month at Kendal I have felt so much stronger and better in all ways.

November 16
I went down to the cellar this morning. This was Bob's domain, and I never go down there without thinking of him and glancing over toward the corner where his work bench stood and where he spent so many happy hours with his silver work. If not silver, he always had some woodworking project going.

Today I had a purpose down there. I went over to the corner where my hooked-rug wools live, and in a large box next to them were a couple of zippered plastic bags filled with cotton material in tiny patterns. This is my patchwork quilt department. I took my materials upstairs and settled in the living room to cut out squares. Next I knelt on the living-room rug and designed my pattern, pinning the squares on a large sheet, and then I began sewing them together.

Bob always used to read to me while I made patchwork quilts or hooked rugs, or sewed anything. We always had a book going. Sometimes two, and would fit the book to our mood of the moment.

Will I ever stop thinking about Bob? Whatever I do, I am always remembering how I did it when he was living. Maybe I will never stop recalling times with him. Maybe I don't even want to. But I believe it will be helpful when I am no longer in this house. I can see Bob sitting in his favorite chair, reading, with the light on beside him. The glow from the lamp reflecting on his white hair and his face, and his hands holding the book.

I guess I have a lot to be thankful for in the number of years we had and all the moments like these reading-aloud times, and countless other experiences that we shared and lived through together.

December 15

The past few weeks I have spent going over the house room by room, closet by closet, and sorting out things I don't need and haven't used for a long time. Anything I haven't used for a year must go, I decided. Of course, right away I found exceptions to this. But on the whole I got rid of a lot of things. Sent them to the hospital exchange.

Joan and Jeffrey will be here in a week or so, and we

shall be together again for the second Christmas since Bob died. I am getting the house ready for them and cooking ahead and putting things in the freezer.

December 29
What a beautiful Christmas we had together. As usual, Jeff drove all night to get here. Before he came, Joan and I tackled the kitchen, going over all the cupboards and drawers and getting rid of things I didn't use or need. Jeff, with his car, could take back a great number of items he wanted, and also things for Joan. Soon after he arrived we had him deeply involved in helping sort and decide.

This Christmas was much better than last. I am at last free from that awful heaviness in my body that I had for so long. Since the cruise and the trip west, actually since my month at Kendal, I have been feeling much better in all ways. I have much more physical energy these days. And no more ailments!

Joan and I had many a good long talk about Crosslands and the wisdom of my going there. She feels it is a very good idea. I am really becoming more and more convinced that it is the place for me. Of course, I can still change my mind at any time. Once I give the house to a realtor to sell, then I will be finally committed. I will have to do this some time in January to give him a good leeway for selling it.

The Third Year

January 25

Finished the patchwork quilt today.

Made a trip down to the cellar to get my hooked-rug material out.

I wonder why I love rug hooking? It is such a simple-minded occupation. You just reach your hook through the backing and draw up a little loop, and then do it over and over.

Perhaps the charm lies in seeing the pattern form. My quilt has been a great help to me this winter so far. There are so many vacant intervals in the day. It is too soon to get dinner. It is too early to go to bed. I have a half hour before I go and get my hair done. All these time interludes are for handwork, whatever the kind you like most to do. It is in the spaces between activities that I tend to travel the same mental track I have been on nearly two years now of missing Bob, of being lonely. My handwork fills these intervals with happy and constructive feelings and thoughts.

I am discovering that I haven't the energy to keep going all day, nor the inclination to be with people all day, so I always have some handwork available. I seldom sit and hook for more than an hour, or make quilts or whatever handwork I have beside me. More likely, it will be a half hour, or fifteen minutes. Just a few minutes means one square added to the next, or with my rug, in ten minutes there will be one new flower added. It is amazing the large projects that evolve and complete themselves from a number of short segments of time. I don't know what I would do without my handwork.

I also have started a little patchwork pillow for my grandchild Mandy. It is made of scattered little shapes of cotton material, no two cut the same size or shape. I do embroidery where the pieces meet one another. Making this is a delightful pastime, along with my quilt and my rug. I will have the pillow completed in another few days. With something to pick up and sew, I am more generally content.

I believe having a lot of interests and pursuing them is a great help in working your way through a grief situation.

February 4

My next-door neighbors are in the real-estate business. It was at their house for dinner that I told them they could put my house on the market, realizing as I did so that now I was committed. I had sort of a sinking feeling. But still I feel it is a right decision.

How I wish Bob were here to advise me. After we'd talked it all over I would feel sure in my mind as I always did after our big decisions. But now I must decide alone. And I guess I have. This is it. After I've told the men to go ahead I can't do any more backing and filling.

In bed that night, I tossed and turned to the refrain of "The House is For Sale—The House is For Sale."

In a queer sort of way, I felt a traitor to the place. Here this house, designed so lovingly by our architect son,

Bob, had housed us and delighted us for over seven years, and I was leaving it and going to let others take over.

February 15
Tonight friends came over to have dinner with me. We had a wonderful fire that we sat before as we talked. What a good evening we had. The fire was cheerful and comfortable. I loved making it and was quite proud of how well it burned. Last fall, when I started to make fires, I felt rather insulted that I had to carry wood and build a fire. I had never built one before, peculiar as that sounds. Fires and woodpiles were Bob's world, not mine.

Then, after he died, I began to need to make a fire if I wanted one. At first, each one I made gave me more anguish than pleasure. They were stubborn and went out, those fires built of resentment and dislike. But one day my fire caught, burned beautifully, and I was greatly encouraged. Gradually, remembering what Bob did, I sort of got the hang of letting air in in the right places and starting with enough paper. These fires slowly got better and better until now I can build a successful one, and I am proud of the fact. I love to light one. We can't burn a fire in our grate when the wind blows by the nature of mountain air currents and our location. I used to hope the wind would blow so I wouldn't have to make a company fire. But lately I honestly hope it won't blow because I love making them.

It is the same with wrapping packages. Bob always prepared packages to be mailed. How skillfully he did it. I would contribute my finger on the first knot occasionally, but no more. Now it is such a joy for me to wrap a package. I sent Miles's quilt to him after I had finished it, and was very proud of my neat, well-wrapped parcel (as well as the patchwork quilt within).

I look upon fires and packages as two small but very significant milestones on my new path, the path that I am walking alone.

February 22
I like to tend my plants indoors. Nothing is quite the same as having your hands in the warm spring earth, but next best is caring for house plants. Feeling the foliage. The firm vitality of each leaf. It is like being in touch, close touch, with nature, with the forces of life itself. These forces abound in nature outdoors. But when we cannot get out much it is a help to be close to these forces in the small way we are when we water a philodendron.

February 23
Working in the garden is one of my most powerful reserves for when I have low moments. You are allying yourself with the strength of the earth when you plant a seed, cultivate, weed, or work in the garden. There is a response when you merely touch something that is growing that you get no other way. The sun is shining down, the breeze is blowing through the pines, a cardinal is singing somewhere. There is a robin hopping through the holly, and now down to the myrtle. Something fresh and alive flows through our veins when we relate to outdoors again after winter weeks of being inside. When it is very cold the best reason to go out is how good it feels to come in again. But now, today, the early spring weather

draws out all my reserves. I respond to nature in a subtle and indescribable way, and feel nature respond to me.

February 25

I guess each one of us must figure out his own special pattern for picking up low spirits. Low spirits will come. It is much better if we can lift them before they get too far down. Just when they begin to sink is the time to bring out your reserves. Mine are numerous. At this time of year they include hooking my rug. I love color, and the bright colors of all the wools are a real feast for my eyes. It gives me a good feeling just to look at my wools, all hanging on a wire circle on the stand that Bob made me. Handling the colors and wools is a joy. I like watching the pattern form, seeing the different colors find their true places. I love it, and it lifts my spirits.

Another occupation I draw out of the reserves is making desserts—meringues, sponge cake, lemon pudding, bread. I can lose myself kneading bread. You are handling life when you handle the dough. You can feel the elasticity develop and the dough grow firm beneath your hands. Kneading is dealing with life in a very positive and constructive way. It takes a few hours to make bread, and a whole morning is gone before I know it when I set out my organic flours and the yeast and grease the pans and prepare for my two large and two small loaves of bread. This is what I make at one time. The small loaves are handy to take to a dinner hostess.

Perhaps best of all for getting myself out of the doldrums is writing letters. I have a large and lovely correspondence, which I cherish. Often I will finish my supper by 6:30 or 7:00. Then I bathe and get ready for bed.

Settled with lots of comfortable pillows and my clip-board, pen, and a pile of letters to answer, I begin. I have friends in Europe, the north, family in the west, people I know and love all over the place.

When I write a person it is very much like a visit with him or her. Well, almost. Next best, shall we say. So I settle with reams of nine-by-twelve sheets on my clip-board. This is for a long letter to someone I know well enough to be informal. For half an hour or an hour, if it is a long letter, I am in Europe, in Switzerland, with my friends to whom I write there. I am totally outside myself as I share with my friends what I have been doing and reading, what I have been thinking and feeling. Perhaps I have heard some good lectures and in sharing them I hear them over again. When you write you live twice. Each experience I recount I relive in the telling of it to special people.

When I settle down for some letter writing—some good visiting with friends—even the worst doldrums flee, to be gone for good, or at least until the next time.

This evening I feel my spirits a little down—just beginning to sink, so I shall hook my rug for a while and then settle in bed and write letters. I'll not get into cooking tonight. I just feel like communing with some of my friends. In a single evening I may visit New York City, San Francisco, Paris, and the lake country in England. What riches are mine for this evening!

February 27
You are never alone in a garden, nor hardly ever lonely. There are birds going about their business. Three squir-

rels are skittering up the trunk of an oak and chattering to each other, or maybe to me. A marvelous beetle is crawling over the ground just here beside me, as if to see if I have planted the parsley correctly. I sowed a good row of this along in the semishade part of the garden. When I turned up the earth I came across several earthworms. Raking up some of last fall's leaves, I discovered beneath them several clumps of daffodils in bud. We are having a most unusual but very welcome warm spell. It is 78 degrees, and the sun is streaming down.

I am tying up more clematis, which has sunk to the ground in a heap of tangled stems, but at the stem joints green leaf buds are visible. While I am trimming some espaliered magnolias on our fence the squirrels are dashing up the maple tree next to the woodpile, chasing each other up and down the trunk and springing from branch to branch when they get up high. As they run down the trunk they cheerfully knock off several pieces of kindling that lay along the top of the woodpile. One falls on the ground, just missing a crocus bud. Chickadees are chirping and, along with a purple finch, are hopping on and off the bird feeder, pausing now and again for a sip of water at the tiny pool there.

And all the while the lizards are climbing up and down the handle of the broom that hangs outside against the house wall by the living-room door to the terrace. They slide around out of sight behind the broom handle when they see me. Then, as I move off, I look back over my shoulder and see them venturing forth again.

No, you can never be lonely in a garden. Too much happens there.

March 2

Every now and then a very peculiar feeling comes over me. I go into a dead stop. I catch myself standing at the window in the kitchen or somewhere and just staring, my mind a perfect blank. I am not seeing what I look at. I have no initiative, no urge to do anything, go anywhere, move at all, not even think. A kind of lethargy fills me, mind, body, and spirit. Several minutes slip by, and I am hardly aware of time.

Pretty soon it is time to get a meal, go to bed, go out and get the mail from the mailbox, take a walk, or go grocery shopping. I do what is to be done quite automatically, with no feeling or enthusiasm.

I used to have these times often the first few months and up to a year after Bob died. Then they lessened.

This afternoon, here it is nearly two years later, and I had one really bad dead period. I know now that it is like a wheel I need to make go forward. Once I start moving I gather a little momentum, and it is easier to keep going. This afternoon I began by baking a sponge cake. It came out beautifully, and this gave me a kind of forward push. I next went outside and cleaned out our tiny pond. It has cracked in the winter and can't be refilled until it is repaired. I phoned our builder, and he said he would come up and cement it again. Then I came in and wrote checks to pay bills. I washed some stockings and odds and ends that needed hand washing. I called a friend who had just come home from the hospital and had a phone visit with her for fifteen minutes or so.

At these times I can't read because I can't concentrate. It is something active I need—something where I can see results. There are my piles of envelopes of paid bills that cheer me some. There are my clean clothes hanging in the bathroom. And in the kitchen the sponge cake is in a tube pan cooling upside down on a bottle of sherry. So I look about at my achievements. Little enough in the general scheme of things, but part of my daily living needs are met by these simple activities. At the same time, things are thus started moving forward in my thinking. I have passed another milestone and turned aside from another dead spell that enveloped me.

I am surprised that I still have these very bad moments now, two years later, when so much else is so much better.

March 4

I miss a man's conversation these days. Most of my life is spent among women. It is so interesting to hear men's comments on world affairs, and I don't have much opportunity for this. When I ask my friends who are couples for dinner I revel in the chance to hear what the husband thinks about what's going on in the world—the news—the world in general.

April 6

These last weeks many people have seen the house. And today the place was sold.

A terrible weight like lead settled in my middle. I smiled and talked with the new owners. (They did not want to move in for several months, giving me ample time.) But my mind traveled back nine years to when Bob and I stood in the same living room, captivated by the overall house plan and the simplicity of it. Then I began remembering when we had our house-blessing ceremony after the house was completed and we had been there a few weeks. Our son Bob had designed us a complete remodeling job, and after it was all finished we had the house-blessing ceremony with a few close friends and a minister friend, one of our nearest and dearest. He devised a simple and beautiful ceremony in which he blessed the workmen who built the house for us; the community; our friends, and us. It was a solemn and moving experience, and afterward I felt that we properly belonged to this newly built house, and it properly belonged to us.

April 8
What a terrible day. Every few minutes the refrain ran through my head, "The House is Sold," "The House is Sold." In a queer sort of way I felt I had let Bob down.

Come, come, I told myself sternly. Are you a prisoner of a pile of lumber? Wall-to-wall carpet, and a beautiful fenced-in garden? Life is ever changing, and our needs in one period of living are not necessarily the needs of the next period.

I am starting a new life, and this house and Tryon are not to be a part of it. My new chapter will occur in a fresh and different location. I have reasoned this all through and decided it is a wise move, and the thing for me to do. I am back in the same position frequently these days where my mind and emotions do not agree. That is my problem.

Perhaps in a few days I will get used to the idea that the house is sold, and be more accepting of the fact.

April 10

If I can just keep moving forward. If I can just *keep moving*. Things are better. Some days I seem to settle into the same old static state. I don't want to do anything much. But if I just put one foot in front of the other and do things, get the meals, shop for food, answer mail, garden a little, make a necessary phone call or two. If I can just do the simple everyday things all through the day, it helps.

When Bob and I were together we each needed the other. And now there is no one who really needs me, I realize. Tomorrow will be just as good for almost everything I do. It gives me a bad time to realize that there is nobody who really needs me. The children and grandchildren love me, and we all get on well together, but they get along very well without me.

I believe it all comes back to *me*. I needn't feel sorry for myself, but rather realize that, true, no one needs me in the way Bob used to need me, but in a different way. Jane needs me, and I need Jane. But basically and quite definitely, I need me.

I am important to *me*. Very. I am alone, an independent unit, and a very important one, as is each one of us.

It is a sense of our own importance that we lose when we lose a mate. As Bob's wife I had a certain stature. Now, alone, I need to place the same value on myself, but it is different and sometimes difficult.

A sense of my own worth, of being somebody in my own right, this is what I need to feel. Totally apart from Jane or any of my favorite people, friends and family, I must be an important person to myself. An awareness of this puts things in their proper place and keeps me moving forward as a result of my own impetus and initiative. Not pushing myself forward, but moving naturally and easily, impelled from within, not without.

April 15
I have gained a great deal of confidence in driving these last two years. It shocks me to realize how out of practice I had become at the time Bob died. I, who drove from Connecticut to Los Angeles by myself when our first grandchild was born, had become fearful of driving, even around Tryon. What a slip back that was. And driving at night—I didn't like it a bit. Even driving the half hour to Spartanburg by day was something far beyond me.

That was then. But now, feeling so much better about it all, I am thinking that one day soon I shall drive to Spartanburg by myself. I have driven it a couple of times lately with Jane. She has been so patient and is always willing to accompany me when I want to go there for errands. Sometimes I drive, and sometimes she does. My apprehensions have pretty well vanished.

I like driving again now. I feel my erstwhile confidence and joy in getting around places returning. Thank goodness. I have driven since I was sixteen. I *should* feel at home at the wheel. More and more now I feel comfortable going places after dark. The lights of other cars no longer confuse me as they did two years ago.

Yes, I am about ready to drive to Asheville, forty miles up the mountain, or to Spartanburg, which is thirty miles southward.

April 16

I have been turning over in my mind the possibility of going to Kendal again this summer for a month. Perhaps July this year. I had such a good time last season, I think before I move up it would be valuable to be there. I could explore the area by car, find out what is where, and learn the best places to shop for various things. Find a nice nursery where I can get plants for my miniscule garden. Also, I can enjoy the friendships I made last summer and do some more painting. In addition to all these reasons, Tryon is very hot in July.

About a week ago I wrote Mrs. Compton to see if I could have her apartment again. I was happy there last summer, and I should love it again this year. I just received a letter from her today saying that I may rent it for July. I am very pleased.

Then when I get back I will have just six weeks before the move. That will be time enough if I do a lot now before I go up to Pennsylvania. I try to achieve something every day in the way of sorting, disposing of, clearing out, making decisions of what to keep and what to get rid of. What to take and what to leave.

April 23

It was very difficult to work in the garden alone all last summer. For fifty years Bob and I had worked the soil together. We both loved it. This was one of the many interests we shared. It is difficult now to be out there alone in a way. But I feel much better about it this year than last. This year I am beginning to feel again the great healing that is in the earth. To be weeding, cultivating, tending plants again brings me closer to the forces of nature, and I feel I am touching and being one with something much greater than I—with something that gives me new strength and courage some way. I could not feel this last year. But gardening today lifts my low spirits, and they still are low at times these days. This was Bob's last garden. The last thing he did on our place. I believe he would like to think I plant and tend it carefully and with love.

I feel nearer to Bob in a garden than anywhere else, almost.

May 2
Just one week ago today I took the afternoon plane to New York City. Joan met me at the airport, and we went to her tiny, compact apartment in Greenwich Village, where I stayed for a week.

I had lunch with an old friend I hadn't seen since Bob died. How important old friends are. We had so much to say to each other as we shared all that had happened to us both these two years. New friends are wonderful, stimulating, exciting, but old friends with whom you have shared ups and downs are especially heartwarming.

We talked about Bob and her husband, who had died a few years before Bob. We shared ways of adjustment we had each discovered, and the crises and trials of this period of changing over to life alone. She has done so well. She thought I had, but I felt she was ahead of me. She teaches classes in Italian at the New School, and studies there herself. Each year several new courses. When you are learning something new you can't grieve so much. How right she is.

Great as my week was with visits to museums, the

ballet, and wonderful talks with Joan, it was good to get home.

It is very pleasant to be in my own bed, to hear the breeze rustling the leaves outside the window, and the sound of the brook rushing along its sandy and stony bed, and the distant sound of a train whistle somewhere in the mountains.

May 9
Betty and I went to Tanner's dress shop this morning. We both bought some new dresses, and it gave us quite a lift. We drove home in the best of spirits. How different from last fall. I remember when I came to Tanner's then I couldn't want a thing, nor care at all.

May 11
Jane is in the hospital.

It had unsettled me terribly to see Jane so far from herself and in such pain and not be able to do anything about it. If only she were out of pain, I thought, as I sat on the terrace under the stars. Perhaps that is what we need to do in life—make our peace with the "if only's" we come up against.

If only Bob hadn't died.

If only my move was behind me.

Bob did die. My move is ahead of me, and much to do still to prepare for it. And Jane is in great pain, and all my love and caring doesn't lessen it one little bit. Life has for each of us a goodly number of "if only's" and we may as well accept them because there is nothing we can do to prevent them.

Pretty soon I went to bed. I lay there unable to sleep

with thinking about Jane. The tears rolled out and dampened the pillow.

It was past midnight when I finally dropped off to sleep.

May 17

In a sense, Jane is where I was a year ago. She is having to give up and give over and give in; to let go and let medical science take over just as I had to. It was hard for me to give in at first, and it was hard for her, too. But the difference lies in the fact that her problem now is a lot more serious than mine was last year (when I was in the hospital for treatment). Also, she has more of a background of belief in natural foods. It is more difficult for her to give in to medical science. She has really done wonderfully.

Jane is a giver, and it is not natural for her to receive. She even resisted the idea of a blood transfusion. But before she was conscious after the operation, blood was dripping into her veins. Dr. B. said she had lost a lot of blood and must have the transfusion and, happily, she let them continue. But she did sputter a little to me about it. I said that, after all, some nice person had been willing to give her the blood—she should be happy about it. Also, that she would never know what interesting traits came with it. Maybe a lot of nice new ones that she could use.

She said she hadn't thought of it that way.

June 3

These days there are two ways I think about Bob. One, I think about him with a kind of ache of loneliness, a deep yearning to feel again his arms about me, to feel his hair, his shoulders, the back of his neck. I long to hear him laugh, see the sparkle in his eyes, hear his voice, see him walk in the door.

The other way of thinking about Bob, I feel proud and happy to have been married to him for fifty years. To have had his love and affection and caring through the early years of marriage when the three children were babies; to have had his understanding and wisdom as the children grew older and needed the guidance he could give them. And then to have the years of retirement we had, traveling, exploring Europe, enjoying our home. I feel proud and happy to have been his wife for all those fifty years; fifty years of growing together, meeting challenges, disagreeing, agreeing, working through things, and always together.

This second way is how I feel today and now. And when I feel this way I want to stand tall and breathe deeply. I feel good through and through.

June 5

Perhaps there are two answers—no, there are never answers, only directions, so I'll say there are two directions for making the kind of adjustment I am struggling to make. Involvement and commitment. The days that are the best are the days when I am involved and committed to my activities. Just doing things and going places to keep busy is not the solution. But involvement and commitment are two important states to cultivate during this period. It doesn't matter what you are involved in and committed to. It may be doing volunteer work at the hospital, or it may be making a loaf of bread, or it may be digging in the garden. If you are sufficiently with any activity it will be a building, helping experience.

The difficulty lies in the fact that your main involvements and commitments at first and in the early months are with what has been, what might have been, with how terribly lonely you are; in other words, with your own thoughts about these states. The deeper you are in such thoughts and feelings the more you amplify them and hold yourself back. Success lies where the action is. The action which you may have to start with stern determination, and just because it is some kind of doing something. But soon, and if you will let it, the action takes over. Into your participation creeps a bit of involvement, then the activity does itself, and you just follow along. It is this kind of doing, when you are altogether with it, that helps rebuild your confidence, your love of life, your peace and contentment. It is this kind of being thoroughly involved that keeps you in today and tomorrow and leaves yesterday behind.

What we need more than anything is to leave yesterday with all of its "if only's," "maybe I could have's," "maybe I should have's," and "why didn't I's." Leave them all in a heap, deserted in favor of the ongoing sense of joy in the now and peace in what will come and what will be.

June 6
In this house I tend to live in yesterday, but I am learning gradually to live in today and tomorrow. I believe this will be easier at Crosslands.

My life with Bob is built into the very walls of this

place. There was the day we came in to find the newly-put-up grass cloth on the living-room wall all crinkled. We were horror-struck, but this is what it does in the process of drying. Afterward, when it smoothed out, we laughed together about our acute concern.

Bob is in the garden at every turn of the path. Here are the bloodroot plants we dug up together one day up in the mountains, when we had brought a picnic and hiked, ate lunch, and dug plants.

Thoughts of Bob are in the very furniture. Here are the ladder-back chairs we bought unfinished when we drove up beyond Asheville exploring one day. Bob finished them so beautifully. They feel smooth as silk.

Even in the vistas from the windows. Yes, we stood here in this window in the early spring the first year the magnolia bloomed and studied the new leaf buds with the field glasses to see which were flower buds and which leaf buds. The former are fatter, and the difference is plain.

It is all Bob and me and the things we did together. Memories at every corner. Memories that awaken the past, that invite me backward through time. And this isn't my needed direction now. I must face forward, move forward.

Perhaps one day I will learn to bring these and a hundred other memories of Bob's and my life together forward into the present as sustenance to draw riches from. Memories can bring not only pain but happiness too. They can be a source of joy, of continuing refreshment, adding strength and meaning to the life of today and bringing hope and confidence into the plans for to-morrow.

As you move forward, taking your memories with you, they tend gradually to change from anguish to peace, then slowly to joy. But this is not so at first. At first memories flood in enough to drown you and bring only pain. This suffering just has to be lived through somehow. There are no rules for getting through it. We muddle along as best we can, each in our own pattern of being. But there comes a day when they undergo a metamorphosis, these recollections from way back. They change from stones around your neck that would drag you down, to treasures that you turn this way and that in the palm of your hand, letting the sunlight of appreciation shine on them that you may best see and know all their fine facets.

My memories were at first only heavy stones. But now, while some days they are still stones, other days they are true treasures.

June 9

Jessie and Malcolm Wiltshire, who bought our house, came for dinner. They came to Tryon for a few days to measure for curtains and furniture and see to a few things. I wondered if it would be as difficult as the tea party we had when they bought the house. It wasn't at all difficult. I have such a good feeling about them here. This place has seen a lot of love, and it will, I feel, see a great deal more with them living here.

I am beginning to feel sort of detached from this house. When my eyes rest on a piece of furniture here or there I am envisioning it in my new apartment rather than where it stands at the moment.

June 12

I believe it will be easier to put my new home together than to take this one apart as I am doing now. As I prepare each room for the movers, it—the room—develops a sort of impersonal, unlived-in appearance and feel. I have Bob's study ready, my bedroom, and the living room. Everything that needed to be cleared out is cleared out so as to let the movers come in and take over. When I thought about doing this a year ago, it seemed a monumental, insurmountable task. But now, as I do it, it isn't bad at all. It is sort of businesslike, and I feel quite efficient and content after I have fixed a certain area.

My study, the dressing room and my clothes, the kitchen and dishes, the Sunrise Room, the bathrooms are yet to be done. I go over each cupboard, drawer, and closet and take out what I want to part with or what I must part with because I haven't room.

When I get to my apartment in Crosslands and begin to arrange things to be lived in and with, it will be a lot easier and pleasanter. Putting together is always more satisfying than taking apart.

June 20

Occasionally these days I feel as if Bob were close beside me as I make decisions. I have a kind of inner knowing, as if he were suggesting what directions to take, how to meet the challenges that come along, which way to turn when I reach a crossroad. Sometimes I sense his presence as I make choices, little and big, that seem right.

At the same time, I feel the independence of standing alone and having confidence and knowing myself where I am going and being sure of the rightness of the direction.

June 26
In three days I shall leave for my month at Kendal. My two suitcases are packed. I am all ready inwardly and outwardly to have a change of scene and be in a different place for a little while.

July 14
This month at Kendal is an expanding one. Everything opens out, unfolds, and unrolls before me. New people and new experiences. The life of this community is a caring one. I see all around me one person caring for another. Yet we all have our privacy and opportunities to be alone in our individual apartments. As quickly as you meet your neighbor he becomes someone you wish well, and about whose well-being you soon come to care.

In Tryon, I am living in an epilogue. An epilogue to the wonderful six and one-half years Bob and I were there together. But an epilogue with an ending, a door closing, a book finished. And this is how I feel about my life in Tryon. It is over and done with, and for that reason I am no longer happy there. It is a life turning backward, thinking backward.

I must take my grief, my low moments, my static times when I seem to be waiting and not moving in any direction. I must take these different moods and carry them forward into a new life. I have with me and inside me my sadness, my grief—yes, but more than these, I have the future, the whole of it unrolling before me like a magic carpet. I have my new life with its potentials, its possibilities. And on this new path I have promises to keep. Some days, lately, I am aware of a Power greater than I, of a Power that lies deep within me and that is with me always, whether I am recognizing it or not. It is there in good moments and difficult ones. This Power is something to lean on, to depend on, to listen to for guidance.

Sometimes I sense Bob's spirit, which after fifty years of married life I came to know so well, walking with me, invisible, but there.

An awareness of his strength and wisdom comes to me. His caring reaches me. Wherever he is, he cares, and this caring keeps me in balance, keeps me willing to cope, to step forward, to enter my new life with a degree of acceptance and contentment.

The sense of the presence of a Power greater than I will always be there. This Power is in me, it is in others. It comes to me in moments of my own inner stillness. When I feel the firm resilience of a growing plant in the garden, something in me quickens, and I sense a close relationship with nature, with all that grows, and I am aware of my connectedness with all that lives and moves and breathes.

July 21

The management called and offered me an apartment with a better location and view than the one I had selected. I am very happy with the change.

July 25

It is midnight. To my complete amazement, there is a mockingbird singing in a treetop somewhere. I am sitting here listening as I sip hot milk and molasses. This is one of those nights. When I do not go to sleep readily I sometimes think it is because messages are coming to me that I need to heed.

As I listen to this melodious tune in the summer night, I am thinking about my stay here, my life in Tryon, and my imminent move. I am wondering, are there any messages?

It is very dark; we are in the dark of the moon. You cannot see where you are going outside. There are stars in the heavens, but tonight they do not shed light or point a way. But the mockingbird continues to sing from his treetop, caroling his many-themed song.

What does he say? Perhaps he is warning to wait for the dawn of a new day before you venture far, lest you lose yourself in the dark night. The new day will come, and with it all things new, a fresh beginning. It is midnight, the moment when the old day ends—and now, minute by minute, hour by hour, the new day approaches.

It will still be dark for many hours yet, but the new day is on the way in spite of appearances. The new day will come, and nothing can prevent it.

Is the message for me? To have faith in my future?

I am reminded of Rabindranath Tagore's definition of faith.

"Faith is the bird that feels the light and sings when the dawn is still dark."

August 14

My books are packed. Those to go to the Crosslands library, where I can read them but don't have to house them; and those special favorites for my apartment, where I shall have bookcases built. I am keeping the poetry, nonfiction, and inspirational books, and parting with a lot of the novels, which you look back at less often.

The house begins to look a little sad without any books on the shelves, but it is a wonderful feeling to have them packed. I want to do all I can ahead so as to keep from getting frazzled the last few weeks.

Why should a move be hectic and an awful and difficult experience? I think I shall see if I can make mine unique. Why can't it be an exciting challenge, an adventure, and stimulating? Why not? I may not succeed in having a unique and happy move, but I am going to try.

One of the secrets, I have decided, is to do everything ahead. I am writing out change of address cards these days. I make lists, lists of everything, what furniture goes with me from each room, what areas I still have to sort through.

August 18

It is two and a half years since Bob died, and still I have times when I feel pretty miserable, days when I miss him achingly. I believe I am realizing now that grief is something you must learn to live with. Will it be with me always? Will I always be subject to being caught by some phrase, the sight of a familiar object, or a situation which will bring back my thoughts to Bob and my loss? Probably yes, and I have recently begun to suspect that this is the way of it—that grief is to be my companion forever.

Location doesn't affect it, make it more or less. I had some just as bad days at Kendal as in Tryon. Grief is something built into me that I am ever conscious of, sometimes more keenly than others. My job is to make a companion of grief, to learn to get along with it, to live my life in its presence without being thrown by it.

People often speak of one who has lost a husband or a wife as "getting over it." I have come to the conclusion that you never get over it. You can learn to get along with it in time, but you never get over it the way you get over the flu and are the same as before. I am sure that I will never be the same as before. Grief and sorrow over the loss are ever there, ever present, ever capable of bringing to a beautiful day or a good experience a moment of pain. One lives closer to pain always after losing a mate. There are times when you are involved and committed to some piece of work, but you are ever vulnerable to the sudden appearance of a painful memory, an unexpected stab of loneliness. These times are always there beneath the surface to be brought up to consciousness by a word, a fragrance, a bar of music, or a sunset.

We continue our activities in the presence of these difficult moments, and perhaps this is what is important and needed—to carry on, never shoving aside the bad moment that crops up, but facing it, accepting it, taking it with you, and still carrying on. I don't think grim determination to put the thought aside is effective either. You cannot force grief aside, you cannot stamp on or overcome it by strength.

You can only accept it, see it for what it is, and carry it with you into your current activity, accept it as a permanent part of your day. This way it fits into the picture of your life. Because it finds its place in the scene, it belongs, it becomes part of the furniture of your soul. Fitting into place, it doesn't stand out to be stumbled over and knocked into all the time. It has its location and stays in it. You can conduct your affairs cheerfully in the presence of grief, and even after a time, I feel sure, with gradually increasing joy in your heart.

August 28

How exciting it really is to be commencing anew at this point in life! After I move, my day will be lived in a different pattern. My whole life will have a new design. Everything about it will be different—everything. This is both stimulating and thought-provoking to consider.

I can hardly wait to see who will be my new neighbors, the people on either side of me. Will they be couples? Will they be single men and women? And what will they be like? How can I wait until September 19 to know, and actually they may not have moved in by the time I get there. I may have to wait longer.

How will my furniture look in the new environment, in a new arrangement? Will I be able to achieve my goal of an uncluttered apartment? This I must have, and if I am taking too many things I will have to dispose of some once I am settled in. I want my three rooms to be cozy and inviting and not with wall-to-wall furniture.

I am still working to make my move more of an adventure and fun than trial and tribulation. Can I do this? So far so good.

All is nicely in hand as of now.

So many of my friends have asked me for lunch and dinner. My days until Labor Day are quite full. After that I won't make any social engagements because I need to be free in my mind and as to time for the unexpected things that turn up at the last minute.

People are being so dear these last weeks. I shall leave here happy in some respects but sad in others. I will be sad to leave my very wonderful friends who have helped so much lately with their affection and caring and by standing by. Glad because I know it will be easier to live my new life in a place that is new and different. Also, I will no longer be in this house alone, which I have found so difficult all along.

September 1
The inconsistency of humans!

As the time draws nearer for my actual move, I find myself thinking a lot about the meaning of it all. And here occasionally I still find myself tangling with my love-hate relationship with this house. My mind and emotions still do not travel on the same track. And when they go in different directions it can be very disconcerting. Here I am now thinking of this house as my one remaining link with Bob, and I am filled with loose, disturbing emotions at the thought of leaving it. My mind tells me I have decided to move. It is a good step and a fine plan. Then my emotions come along and block my thinking with a lot of negative fears about the whole situation.

I guess I wouldn't be human if I didn't at some point do a little backtracking about things in general and have a few qualms about the move. This is just part of the inconsistency. It is probably a little stage fright before the final packing up and actual departure days come. Sometimes when I have qualms I but open the front door and the blast of heat that presses upon me makes me realize how happy I will be to be free from these stifling summers. Then, a mysterious smell of oil seems to fill the air of the carport. Is the car leaking? The furnace oil escaping somehow? Oh hum! This is the sort of thing I won't have to worry about when I move.

Finally, to switch my mood even more thoroughly, I begin thinking how this house isn't really my one and only link with Bob at all. My real link with him is an inner one—one no outer circumstances can break or disturb. It is the awareness I have of what we meant to each other, the life we led together, that I often think about with pleasure. The effect we had on each other—the effect Bob had on me will remain with me always as a basic part of me. These are the links that are worthwhile to dwell on, and with joy.

September 2

I went to see Dr. Palmer today to have my annual physical. All the tests I had done a couple of weeks ago came out normal, and he said I was in fine shape. I felt so good on leaving.

More than just the physical. I had a good talk with him about my move and felt very much better about everything when I left his office. I always feel fine after I see him.

September 7

I have something to confess. I have been so adamant about putting things in Bob's study. That is where things go that I am not taking with me, that will go in the sale. I firmly set things on the cupboard shelves there with a curt feeling of farewell for them. They are out of my life. But are they? The other night I was going to sleep when I began thinking about a little green teapot I had discarded. How could I have? I went in, switched on the light, and rummaged until I found it. And while there, how could I let that tall brown pitcher go? And those crystal goblets? I decided to keep just four of them. Surely there will be room.

Jesse, my married grandson, called a night or two ago to tell me that they could use anything at all that I could not. This gives me a good excuse to draw a few things out of the discard pile. What doesn't fit in my apartment I can give him. I believe it will be easier to get rid of things once I am up there and confronted by lack of space rather than while here trying to imagine how it will be. I am determined I will not live in a clutter. But I can eliminate there what I don't set aside here.

September 11

These days are filled with "lasts." I got my last eggs at Mrs. Jennings—large, lovely brown ones, enough to see me through the coming week until we go, and some left over to leave for the new owners to have for breakfast along with a loaf of homemade bread, and butter. I made my last visit to the bank to cash a check and say good-bye to all my favorite people there. My last visit to see my lawyer and go over final things.

The house looks like a place in transition instead of a home. Large, significant white labels on some of the furniture. Piles of boxes, taped and labeled, in my study; no curtains; no books. I got a burning urge to look up a gnu and an eland in the dictionary and see what sort of creatures they are. And, of course, the dictionary was packed.

Jane came over this morning, and we packed some things. I am going to go into Crosslands with a terrible reputation. We both have been collecting liquor boxes these last weeks. They are sturdy and just the right size. So, printed on my cartons of possessions are "Vodka, It leaves you breathless," Scotch whisky, Kentucky bourbon, sherry, etc. It just happens I don't drink anything more potent than white grape juice, so this approach of mine to Crosslands is a strange one. I trust it will not horrify my neighbors. I think so much about these unknown individuals and who they will be. Who will be on either side of me and above me? This is something I ponder in idle moments. Men? Women? Some of each? Couples? I wonder.

September 17
How strange it felt driving along the highway with Tim, realizing that my furniture and all my belongings were in a van I knew not where. My house was my house no more, and my new apartment not yet mine. I was in a state of transit, neither in one place nor the other, but somewhere in between.

Actually, I felt great coasting over the highway with Tim at the wheel. It was heavenly to have someone else take over. Tim had packed the car so skillfully, winding the clematis around the suitcases, fitting everything neatly in just as Bob used to do.

As we drove along I heard all about his life in California, about the grandchildren's latest doings, and

Jeanne's. We had a wonderful time catching up on a year's happenings.

The farther I got from Tryon the more these last two and a half years seemed to slip away from me. Tryon became the dream place Bob and I came to together in retirement, the place we lived in for nearly seven years. The last two and a half years began to melt away out of memory.

But no, I must not let them go. There was good in them too. It was a period of time I had to go through. A period of accepting and adjusting, an interlude illuminated by a few shining friendships that have become important to me. And now I am leaving them. But no, I am not really leaving them, nor leaving Tryon. Because in a sense the richness of my Tryon life, both with Bob and without him, is built into me, has become a part of me that I shall carry with me wherever I go. I cannot lose or leave these years behind me. They are me, and I them. My time alone and my time with Bob blur together now, and the Tryon segment of my life stands out sharp and clear, has its own relevance, its own entity. In a strange sort of way it all belongs, all belongs to me, and has helped to make me what I am. I will be drawing on this interlude in the years to come, though perhaps not always consciously.

Every period of our lives is a growing one, and now that it is behind me I can see this stretch of years as one of great growth too.

There has been unhappiness, just plain misery. I have been in the depths at times, but there has been a kind of richness even in my depths of despair that I can begin to see from even this distance of a few hundred miles. I have touched the core of aloneness. I have reached the bottom so many times. Then, some way, something, or someone would lift me up.

And now today, as the road unrolled before me and the Blue Ridge Mountains rose on all sides of us, I felt the close of the chapter, the turning of a new page, and the drawing with me into a new phase the heart and core of these Tryon years, the good ones and the difficult ones.

I am different now from when Bob and I drove down to Tryon with all our furniture in the van. Life has moved along. Now is not then anymore. Yet some of the then lives, moves, and breathes in the now, and always will.

We arrived at our destination in the late afternoon. After dinner we went to see my apartment. The curtains were drawn. We couldn't see in, but we could see the ravine and lawn in front of my terrace leading out to it. A fresh breeze blew up to greet us. How beautiful it was. I hadn't counted on this magnificent view of the ravine.

Then it came, that distant honking sound—we both looked up, and there they were, necks outstretched, the great wild Canada geese soaring above our heads. The wild geese flew over our meadow the night before our move from Connecticut to North Carolina, and Bob and I stood spellbound watching them. Now, here I am with Tim just arrived at Crosslands, and here they were, hundreds of them, forming a living V that swerved and bent as they did, its arms stretching and shrinking while they changed course, now this way, now that.

The wild geese that nine years ago had confirmed a change of living pattern, now again fly over. Something momentous has happened to me, is happening. I am beginning a new life. A fresh new page is turning, a new door opening. . . .

October 20
A dazzling Indian summer morning. I am kneeling on the grass where the earth beneath me is gradually cooling, and where now and then a gold leaf drifts down near me. I feel the sun on my back and arms, and it feels good. Beside me on the grass is the paper bag of bulbs that came in the mail a few days ago. I am in the midst of planting them, crocuses, miniature daffodils, snowdrops, scilla, chionodoxa, all those I ordered last month in Tryon. I have a deep sense of joy and fulfillment as I work. And now I sit back on my heels and look around me. Behind me is a ravine, the trees in it are rich gold and copper, and here and there a red dogwood stands out.

Before me is my new little garden. It has just been made by a local nurseryman, and it delights me. The terrace is extended by flagstones, and around the edge of these is a curving bed with evergreens. The feature of it all is a little weeping birch tree swinging streamers of branches tipped with next year's unborn catkins. My little iron turtle stands on the mulch in front of two yews, reaching his head up toward the sun.

Through the open screen door into my apartment comes the fragrance of bread baking. Is there any scent more comfortable and comforting? There lies within me a sense of deep contentment. An hour ago I was kneading bread, feeling the firm, live dough beneath my hands. It is the livingness of bread dough that makes it so much fun to work with. Inside my apartment are all my treasures, my furniture and belongings all arranged and looking, I think, wonderful. The African violets are a feature of the living room; their colors, as I see them now through the window, are glowing in the sun. I am happy with my three rooms. I feel snug and cozy here.

I look into the bag of bulbs at my side. In each firm corm lies a miracle, a wonder of nature to be revealed next spring after the snow has melted and while a warming sun shines down and heats the earth. I like handling bulbs, each one with its crisp brown skin, each one a promise. Here I have a bag full of promises, of beauty, filled with the future, a bright, warm future.

Chickadees are at the feeders my next-door neighbor has. On this special morning I feel one with these cheerful, chirping birds; one with the cold, cold trees all around me whose roots are down deep where the sap lies waiting for spring. I look at the apartments all around me; nearly four hundred people live here in these buildings. We are a community, those I know and those I don't know. No one is a stranger, just a friend I don't yet know. I feel one with my friends from all over whose letters lie in the basket in the living room. So many from far and near have sent me good wishes, love, and blessings. Indeed, I am blessed.

Do I miss Bob in all this? Yes, of course I do, and my aloneness is there underneath everything else. But this is just something I live with now. Something I have made room for in my days and in my life. It may always be there. Those who have lost husbands far longer ago than I have tell me it is always there—the yearning, the missing. But one can make friends with it. And strangely, there is room for happiness, too, at the same time. And while I possess this sense of loss, I am no longer alone.

After two years and nine months, I am again feeling one with my surroundings, one with the friends I know and those I don't know who live here. I am one with my friends and family in far places who send me good wishes. I am one with the earth, the trees, the birds, and now I hear the wild geese flying over. Seven in a V honking gently as they go. Today, all these wild creatures are my friends too.

Walking alone? Never.